$\mathcal{B}$

Briarwood Publications, Incorporated

SHINE FORTH FROM DARKNESS UNTO LIGHT

by William B. Keller

First Published 2000
Briarwood Publications & Sassy Cat Books, Inc.
150 West College Street
Rocky Mount, Virginia 24151

Shine Forth From Darkness Unto Light

William B. Keller

ISBN 1-892614-33-2

Manufactured in the United States of America.

Printed by Briarwood Publications, Inc.

All that I do is for Jill and Will

Photograph of William B. Keller compliments of
Laura Page

Cover design by
Barbara Fleenor Turner

Part One

ONE

Mary Johnson ran along a hot, dusty Tennessee road, clutching a shiny nickel given to her by Miss Packwood, her first grade teacher. Sometimes the hard packed dirt roads were too hot for bare feet, but Mary was too excited to notice on this last day of school. Only students with perfect attendance at the Jefferson Davis Public School for each and every day during the 1924 school year received a reward, and Mary Johnson had earned her nickel. She had struggled through snow, rain, and even a tornado to keep her attendance record, and one January morning climbed out of her bedroom window with a one hundred and three degree temperature to escape her mother's demands that she stay home. Her father had nearly beaten her to death for disobeying, but the record was intact.

Everyone who knew Mary was amazed at how such a tiny little girl, she was the smallest in her class, could be so full of fire and zest for life. Sometimes, when children were in the mood to be cruel, they would call her 'stick girl' because of her thin arms and legs. Such comments were accepted without anger as words had no affect on Mary, but if someone else was being mistreated or abused, a tiny whirlwind struck with the force of a lion. Mary's classmates seldom made the mistake of fighting with her more than once.

Her face was flushed with heat and excitement as she neared home, perfect round circles of red on her cheeks helping her light brown curls to stand out around her pretty face. Running through one of two deep ruts in the path leading nearly a half mile to her house, Mary held her arms out like an airplane's wings and made a sound through her lips like a rumbling engine. She slowed to a walk as she approached the rundown three room cabin which was home, because she saw her father sitting on the front porch with a gallon jug by his side.

Ray Don Johnson had always been a mean drunk, in fact he was usually mean drunk or sober. Mary had learned to avoid him most of the time, and tried to avoid him all of the time when he was drinking corn liquor from his jug. Today, in her excitement, she did not approach home in her typical quiet fashion, studying the situation carefully before approaching the house. Many times Mary slept in the woods all night, slapping at hungry mosquitoes instead of going home to Ray Don's drunken rages and maybe a beating. Now she had no escape because he saw her coming home, and already he was staggering to his feet and beckoning to her.

"Mary, Mary Johnson" he bellowed, pausing to belch a large, foul smelling gas from his stomach, then shouting, "you come up here on this porch right now. Do you hear me girl?"

Her heart dropped to her feet and she could almost feel her ankles thudding as it worked in its new location, but Mary smiled anyway, with her mouth and not her eyes. "Yes Papa, I'm coming" she called out, praying her voice sounded normal instead of tight with fear. She reached the porch and stood on the bare ground surrounding the cabin, just out of her father's reach. "How are you today Papa, is everything all right? I've got some news to tell you" she said, desperately wanting to find him in good humor.

Ray Don was just under five feet, five inches tall and weighed no more than one hundred thirty pounds. He always had what looked like a three day growth of beard, although Mary had never seen him shave. He wore a dirty undershirt which may have been white at some distant time, but now had more motor oil and grease than fabric in its makeup. His jeans were nearly as dirty, the fly of his

4

trousers darkened by urine stains deposited every time Ray
Don passed out drunk, which was often. Most of his teeth
were missing, either from decay or fights, and his light
brown hair was cropped short. He blinked his watery eyes
at her and knitted his bushy eyebrows in anger. "Get up
here girl, like I said" he snapped. "I want you right here
so's I can talk to you." He pointed at a spot by his side.

She had stepped into the trap and it was sprung.
Meekly Mary climbed the porch steps, a condemned
criminal going to the gallows, and placed her dusty bare
feet exactly on the spot indicated by the pointed finger.
Swallowing hard to push back the contents of her churning
belly, she didn't know which was making her sicker, fear or
Ray Don's stench. Squeezing the nickel harder was some
comfort and she kept her eyes down, which seemed to help
when her father was angry. He didn't speak immediately
and she didn't move, sure that this was some sort of test.

Ray Don glared at his tiny offspring with a strange
mixture of love and contempt. She had his coloring and
blue eyes, perhaps reminding him more of himself than
any of his other children, but children were the very fault
of his problems today. He had been the best athlete in the
history of Filmore High, still holding records in track and
baseball. Ohio State had offered him a scholarship to play
baseball until Martha got pregnant, then all offers were
rescinded. Of course that wasn't Mary's fault, it was her
older brother Jeff that his then girlfriend carried in her
womb, but if not for kids he could be playing pro ball instead
of making moonshine and drawing a welfare check. He
took another long drink of liquid fire and shuddered as the
clear alcohol slammed into his nervous system. He belched
again, this time in Mary's face, and smiled when she gagged.
He put his hand around her upper arm, hardly feeling its
thin presence in his palm as he closed his fingers tight
enough to cause just the right amount of pain. "I don't want
you runnin' in the house right now. I got a bill to pay and
your mama's helpin' me with that, so you and I can just

keep out the way for a spell."

Mary didn't answer because she knew he didn't want one, but remained still as stone as the bile rose in her throat to a dangerous level. Her father leaned back in his chair but kept his grip on her arm, which already was making her hand tingle as the circulation was cut off. How long she stood like this was not clear, although it seemed to be hours before she heard the crooked screen door moan as it opened. Immediately the vise on her arm relaxed and she stepped away from Ray Don's side.

Hank Travers stepped onto the porch, sticking his blue work shirt into his pants and then buttoning the fly of his Levi's. An unlit Camel cigarette rested in the corner of his mouth, the round cylinder fitting perfectly into a half moon sore on his upper lip and its twin on his lower lip. He pulled a Zippo lighter from his jeans, snapped the top back as it cleared his pocket, and struck the flint with his thumb as the flame leaped upward, hungrily groping for the tip of the cigarette. Smoke billowed from his nostrils as he pulled a deep drag into his lungs. Standing behind him in the open doorway was Mary's mother Martha.

Years ago Martha Johnson had been pretty, perhaps even beautiful. Certainly as the star athlete in school, Ray Don considered her the prize of the entire school district, at least until he impregnated her. Now she looked drab and beaten, her once shining hair matted and plastered to her head. Four children did not ruin her figure, but she was too thin and pale to still be attractive. She hung her head in shame and fear, the exact posture Mary had learned when dealing with Ray Don Johnson.

"Well now Hank, do you suppose this cancels our little debt?" Ray Don said with a smile. He borrowed money from anyone foolish enough to lend to him, seldom having the funds to repay any loan. Hank was different, his brother being the county sheriff and his father a judge. Debts had to be settled with Hank Travers or unpleasant things would happen.

Travers shook his head slowly and deliberately, smoke billowing from his mouth like a steam locomotive. He walked to the end of the porch and turned toward Ray Don, a smile playing at the corner of his mouth. "Well, I suppose we're only, let's say, half even" Travers said evenly.

Ray Don stood up quickly, the movement causing him to sway slightly and look a bit sick. "I thought we agreed that you would borrow my woman and we call what I owe you square" he cried, blinking his watery eyes in an attempt to focus.

"Well, she wouldn't do what I wanted her to do, so I had to settle for less, and I guess you know that means you have to settle for less too Ray Don." Travers shrugged and winked at Mary, making the little girl back away three more steps.

Ray Don strode over to his wife in two stalking steps. She seemed to shrink into herself, trembling slightly at his nearness. He did not speak to her, only glaring with what appeared to be a mixture of contempt and hatred. His fist shot forward like a piston in an engine and landed with a thud into Martha's midsection. She bent over, air exploding from her lungs in a loud whoosh, and stood with her legs spread like a marionette suspended on strings, arms spread wide as if attempting to fly. Ray Don leaned forward and up as his next punch came from below his waist, an uppercut that landed on his wife's nose. She jerked upright with the force of the blow, the sound of cartilage collapsing and snapping like dry sticks on a fire.

Mary let out a small scream when she heard the sickening sound and saw a fountain of blood spray Ray Don's filthy undershirt, her scalp tingling as he roared an oath when he looked at the dark red stream on his chest. Paralyzed in horror, she could not move her eyes as her father hit her mother again, this time on the very end of her chin. Martha flew backward as if snatched back by a giant invisible hand, crashing against the cabin wall and sliding along its rough surface until she was sitting, head lolling forward, unconscious on the cabin's porch.

Ray Don stepped forward and grabbed Martha's hair, jerking her head upright in preparation to hit her again. Seeing that she was unconscious he loosened his grip and let her chin fall against her chest. He turned slowly, panting slightly and eyes glazed like a madman, looking at Hank Travers.

Hank shook his head and whistled softly. "Man oh man, I don't believe I've ever seen anything like that" he said, a look of admiration and not horror on his face. "Ray Don old buddy, you can just consider us square. That was worth twice what I got inside" he said with a chuckle. "Do you think you killed her?"

Mary gasped at the thought, bringing the men's attention to her, something she knew immediately was another serious mistake. She began trembling as her father ambled toward her, even more frightening with her mother's blood sprayed on him. He was absently rubbing his palms on his chest, covering his hands with red. Mary backed away until her back pushed into the porch rail, trapping her like an animal in a pen.

"Naw, she ain't dead" Ray Don growled as he advanced on his daughter, the same hatred burning in his eyes, "but I might kill her yet if she don't obey me no more." He stepped in front of Mary and looked down at her trembling form. With the speed of a striking rattlesnake he slapped her face with an open hand, the action smearing blood over her face and banging her head on a corner post of the porch.

Mary saw a flash of light, then darkness mixed with shooting stars as the pain exploded in her brain. Her hand flew open, the new nickel dropping to the floor and spinning on its edge like a top. She shook her head in an attempt to chase away the darkness so she could scramble after the treasure, but Ray Don leaned over and plucked it up before it stopped its wild spin. "No" she moaned as it was sucked into his palm.

"Whoa Ray Don" Hank said, "why did you hit the girl?"

"That was just a free bonus" Ray Don said, the far away glazed look still in his eyes. "And here." He tossed the nickel to Hank, who caught it and stuck it into his pocket. "There's some interest on that loan, so's we can really be even now."

"Even up Ray Don, even up. Let's do some business again some day, okay? And next time maybe we can talk about the girl there paying the debt. Think about it." He winked, turned his back, and walked to his car.

Ray Don turned back to Mary, who by this time was staring at her empty hand where the nickel had been. She didn't seem to notice him towering over her, the absent coin holding her attention with the same fascination a flying saucer may have caused. She started back to the present when he grabbed her hair and pulled slowly until her head was forced to tilt back, wide unblinking eyes forced opened with her scalp stretching under the pull of his hands. "Why didn't I think of you before little sis" he muttered, more to himself than to her. He added, "You could be a gold mine for me. You'd like to make your daddy happy wouldn't you girl?"

She tried to swallow the terror that was blocking her throat but her mouth was too dry, causing her tongue to feel thick and rubbery. Finally she was able to whisper, "Yes Papa."

"Good, that's my good Mary" he soothed, loosening his iron grip on her hair but not relaxing his hold completely. "Do you see your mama over there? That's what happens when women disobey me. She was bad, so I had to punish her. I don't like to do that, but you girls have to learn. Do you understand me girl?" His voice grew hard again to emphasize his authority.

"What did Mama do Papa?" Mary asked, curiosity overcoming fear. She stole a glance at her mother, who was stirring slightly and moaned softly as her unconscious mind started feeling the pain. "She looks hurt real bad Papa."

"She'll be all right, but that's what happens when women don't obey. She brought it on herself" he said, his tone soothing again as he offered instruction. "If a man says do something then you do it now and don't ask no questions. You just go on ahead and do it. Now do you think you understand?"

"Yes Papa" she said again. "Papa?"

"What girl" he said.

"You gave Mister Travers my nickel that I earned at school." Tears filled and brimmed her eyes. "I worked all year for that nickel Papa."

His face hardened but almost immediately softened as he formed an idea. "How would you like a dime instead of a nickel girl."

"A dime" she said in an astonished tone. "A whole dime."

Ray Don smiled, three brown teeth showing like little rotted fence posts. "Girl, every time you do what your daddy tells you to do for a friend, you won't get hurt like your mama and I'll give you a dime."

"What do I have to do Papa" she asked, visions of piles of dimes in her mind.

He narrowed his eyes and nodded his head just once, as if making a decision. "You come with me girl." He grabbed her arm again in a firm grip.

Fear leaped forward again. Had she said something wrong? Mary wasn't sure she could take a beating like her mother had just endured. "Where are we going Papa. Did I do something wrong?"

Ray Don propelled her toward the entrance of the cabin, evil determination and lust showing on his dirty face. "You ain't done nothin' wrong yet girl, not a thing, but I'm going to show you what I want and you're going to do it. Then, you get a dime." He paused as the screen door squeaked open and pointed Mary toward her mother. "You don't want that do you?"

"No, no Papa" she cried in terror. "Please don't hit me Papa."

"I won't have to girl if you behave and do as you're told" he growled. "Now git in the house here and I'll start your education." They disappeared into the dark interior of the cabin, like two travelers entering the depths of hell.

TWO

Mary passed out from the pain before her assault was over, but she understood what her father expected and wondered if she could drown herself in nearby Russels Creek. Crawling painfully from her parents' bed, Mary discovered that she was bleeding. Ray Don was gone, she hoped he had fallen into the old dry well in back of the cabin, but probably her luck would not be that good.

She staggered back onto the porch, each step causing more blood to course down her legs, and decided for sure that death would hurt less than this. Her mother stopped Mary from this resolve, and yet she never knew it. Still unconscious and slumped down on the porch, Martha looked so broken that Mary knew she could not add to her pain. Instead of drowning herself she bathed in the creek, sitting in the freezing water until the flow of blood stopped.

When Mary came home she found her mother sitting in a worn overstuffed chair in the cabin's front room. She held a towel to her face and cried quietly, only her trembling shoulders giving away any emotion. Mary walked as quietly as possible over the dirt floor and sat down in a broken straight backed chair positioned in front of her mother. She did not make a sound and Martha continued to cover her face with the damp towel. Time crawled slowly along, shadows moving along the wall as the day became evening. Darkness fell and crickets sang outside before Martha dropped her arms and looked at her daughter in the gloom.

Mary forced herself to not react when she saw her mother's face, its pretty form misshapen and swollen.

Both eyes were blackened, resembling a mask that was hiding from her swollen nose and lips. Only the eyes themselves showed hope, as they blazed through their blackened surroundings with anger and resolve. When she finally spoke, Martha mumbled somewhat because her jaw was too swollen to open, but she made herself understood. "I'm all right baby. I don't want you to worry. He didn't hurt you did he?"

"No Mama, I'm fine. No one hurt me" she lied. Her mama could never know what happened, because what if she blamed Mary for what happened and didn't love her anymore. She resolved to never tell anyone. "I was just scared that you were hurt bad, that's all" she said.

Wincing in pain, Martha slowly stood. "I'm too tough to hurt real bad Honey. I just need a few days out of sight until the bruises heal a bit. Where are your brothers today?" she added almost as an afterthought.

"I haven't seen them Mama" Mary said. She suspected that the boys had either seen their mother as she was beaten or came near the cabin and saw her, bloody and unconscious, on the porch. They would come back either late that night or in the morning, waiting until they were sure Ray Don was gone, which he typically was for some time after hurting someone. "I'm sure they'll be here later" she added, knowing that her mother knew it wasn't true but would accept the fantasy.

"Do we have any food?" her mother asked, moving the focus of her attention to other matters.

"Not much Mama, maybe a few cans of beans and I think a can of tuna. Why don't I get some corn since it's dark. We ought to be gathering in some before it's harvested anyhow." Stealing corn from neighboring fields was a survival tactic for the family, this often being the only food available for weeks at a time. Martha ground the kernels and cooked them on top of the wood stove that served as a cooking surface year round and provided heat during the mild but cooler winter months. Apple trees grew wild all around the area and they planted a large garden for vegetables, but often the stolen corn was the only food available.

"Yes Honey, I imagine we should have some corn" her mother agreed, "but I'd rather the boys go with you. Remember last week your brother Ron just missed getting himself filled with buckshot."

"I know Mama, but I'll be careful, and besides the boys aren't here right now" she reasoned, "and we need the corn."

"I know Mary, it's just that it's stealing and I don't want to send my baby out to do wrong."

"Mama, if we don't take corn we'll starve, and the farmers don't miss it."

The rationalization didn't work but Martha knew they had no choice. Ray Don had gone further than ever before, both in the beating he gave her and bringing his trash friend to her as a payment of debt. Whenever he hurt her she didn't see him for some time, so Martha expected this absence to be longer than usual. Her nose was certainly broken, this being the third time, and hopefully her jaw was just bruised and not broken. A trip to the doctor or the hospital was too expensive and too dangerous. Ray Don might kill her if she got him arrested, an occasional beating being more tolerable than the fear of death.

Mary had changed into a pair of black pants and matching shirt. She also pulled a tattered black baseball cap over her hair, all helping her to blend into the night. She remained barefooted because she did not own shoes. An empty onion sack to carry the corn completed her outfit, the whole effect making her look like a tiny terrorist. "I'm off Mama, I'm going over to the Swanson place cause they're not as likely to miss the corn."

"That's too far Mary" her mother said anxiously. "Let your brothers go to the Swanson's corn field."

Mary rolled her eyes and smiled. "Mama, those lazy old hound dog brothers of mine wouldn't walk no farther than across the street if they didn't have to. They'd strip a field clean before takin' one extra step, so I'm going to get some heat off us in our own neighborhood." Before her mother could answer, Mary ran through the doorway and was almost instantly swallowed by the darkness.

Trudging through the stand of pine trees behind the cabin, Mary's eyes adjusted to night vision and moved toward the distant neighbor's field. She was trying to keep her thoughts from returning to what her father had done, much of her concentration being taken to fight away the ugly memory. A shape leaped from behind a tree like a black ghost, wrapping its arms around her and covering her mouth with one hand. Mary screamed, the sound muffled to a quiet peep, and she thought that for certain Ran Don had come back to teach her again.

She kicked and thrashed like a person possessed, revulsion of his touch bringing on inhuman strength. The creature was talking to her in an urgent whisper, trying to break through the horror that propelled her on. Despite her struggles the attacker finally held her securely, like a fly stuck in a web, until finally she gave up and stopped her fight. Only then did she hear what the urgent whisper was saying.

"Mary, Mary it's me. Mary it's Jeff." Her brother's harsh whisper overcame the sound of her thudding heart. She stopped her struggle and waited as he held her tight, knowing he did not let go because she was trembling. When he loosened his grip she turned slowly, looked into his eyes, and kicked his right shin. "You idiot" she shouted, "how dare you sneak up on me in the dark. I thought about carrying a knife with me, and then I might have cut your heart out Jeff Johnson." She stamped her foot on the ground, more for her benefit than anything, and glared at her grinning brother as he rubbed his leg.

"Well put away your weapons baby girl" he said, "because Ron and Matt are just behind that tree." Even as he spoke her brothers stepped into view, their profiles in the darkness easy for Mary to recognize.

Her brothers were each one year apart in age, the youngest, Matt, being two years Mary's senior. They looked like triplets, each sporting thick red hair that resembled a rusted wire brush. Freckles so closely spaced that at first glance looked like huge splotchy birth marks covered the boys in random patterns. Despite their age differences all three were within one quarter of an inch the same height, and actually it was Matt who was taller. The easiest way to identify them was by personality. Jeff was outspoken and friendly, never having met a stranger. Ron was quiet but offered an easy, genuine smile as a greeting in almost every situation. Matt never spoke and seldom looked anyone in the eyes, expertly shifting his gaze when someone spoke to him. Jeff once told Mary that he remembered Ray Don knocking Matt into a tub of laundry and holding his head under the water for an awfully long time as a punishment. Their mother told a friend that she thought Matt's brain had been hurt because he couldn't breathe, but no one was ever sure. He definitely wasn't social, and even the family didn't know if he couldn't or wouldn't talk.

The four children automatically formed a tight circle, their arms touching and heads tilted inward, enabling them to whisper so softly that even an owl could not have heard them. "Papa hurt Mama really bad" Mary said.

Jeff bristled, his voice tight with anger. "Is she going to be all right?"

"I think so" she said. I sat with her until just a few minutes ago and she seemed to be better, although she's pretty bruised."

"Did he hurt you" Ron asked, leaning forward until their foreheads touched as he strained to see her in the dark.

"No, I'm fine" she lied, forcing back a shudder of revulsion at the memory.

"Is he gone" Jeff asked, reflexively looking over his shoulder in the direction of the cabin.

"Yea, I suppose we won't see him for a while" Mary said, "because this one was really bad." Hastily she added, "What he did to Mama I mean."

Jeff narrowed his eyes suspiciously, obviously not convinced that he was hearing the entire story. "What are you doing out here in the dark?"

"I'm going to the Swanson's field for some corn" she said.

"Why go all the way over there" Ron said with a shrug. "There's plenty of corn right around here, like the Fletcher place."

"Yea, and you just about got your backside shot off the last time you were in their field" Mary reminded him. "Besides, if we strip a field we'll have the sheriff down on us. Right now nobody's going to care about some poor family stealing food so we don't starve, but one of us has to use their head."

Jeff was grateful for the darkness because his face was flushed with embarrassment. The youngest member of the family had the most sense and he was ashamed. "Okay, fine, let's go over to Swanson's for corn, but let's get a move on 'cause my belly's touchin' my backbone now."

With no further comment the children moved as quickly as the darkness permitted toward the Swanson farm. The task took nearly an hour, but they were rewarded by finding a fifty acre field of corn and a dark sky with only a small sliver of moon. Mary filled her bag and the boys stuffed their pockets and made bags by tying the neck and sleeves of their shirts in a knot. By daybreak they were dumping nearly two bushels of stolen field corn into an old potato bin with no lid.

Martha shuffled slowly from her bedroom as she heard her children's excited chatter, blinking sleep from one eye that was not swollen shut. Her jaw was an ugly purple from her lower lip to the top of her neck, and only her cheeks did not show signs or bruising. She looked like a decayed corpse with rouge painted in round circles on her cheeks. A tear ran down her cheek from the open eye when she saw the shock and horror on her children's faces.

"I'm going to kill him" Jeff muttered under his breath, then winced as Mary elbowed him in the ribs.

"You quit talking like that" Mary snapped. "Doesn't Mama have enough grief to deal with without you talkin' stupid." She rushed to her mother's side and guided her to an easy chair, where Martha fell heavily onto the worn cushions. "I'll grind some corn to cook us some breakfast, Matt you run get us some wood for the stove, Ron you fetch some water, and Jeff you shut your mouth." Mary took charge and no one spoke a word of objection.

Grateful for something to do, Ron and Matt rushed to their assigned tasks and Jeff slumped angrily onto a chair. An ancient grinder served well to crush the grains of corn as Mary expertly removed them from the cob with her thumbs and then turned the cracked handle to feed the kernels into the gears. She had a large bowl filled with cracked corn meal by the time the stove was lit and the water was hot.

"You boys wash up before I cook" she demanded, and they dutifully washed the sweat and grime from their hands and faces with a bar of Ivory soap and the warm water on the stove.

Mary covered the top of the stove with a thin layer of ground corn and sprinkled melted lard over the top. Turning the hot concoction over and over with a large spatula, she mixed the lard in for flavor. The boys lined up hungrily with cracked china plates which had come from a grocery store promotion years before, and waited impatiently as the corn cooked. She used the spatula as a serving tool and filled each plate. Without a word the boys ate like ravenous dogs, the hard corn cracking noisily in the quiet cabin as they chewed.

Handing a plate to her mother, Mary frowned when she shook her head in refusal. "Come on Mama" she chided, "you've got to eat or you'll get sick."

Martha pointed to her bruised face and spoke without opening her mouth. "I can't chew honey, my jaw's too sore" she said. "I'll have to give it a day or two I think."

Mary sighed and ate the corn herself, forcing a smile as she chewed the unappealing fare. She hated this, but guessed it was better than starvation. When they finished eating she washed the dishes in the same water they had washed up in and then directed Jeff to throw it on the garden.

"Why me" he groaned. "Ron and Matt can throw it out if they each grab a handle."

"That water's hot and we don't want them getting burned" she reasoned. "Besides, you're the oldest and should be setting an example. And remember to pour the water on the garden so it gets watered and the soap will kill insects."

"Give me a break, I know that already" Jeff said defensively. "You only tell me that every time I dump the water."

"That's because you only pour it on the garden when I remind you" she shot back.

"Quit bickering" Martha said, holding her jaw as she spoke, the slight movement causing pain. "We have enough troubles without arguing about wash water."

Mary felt like kicking herself or her brother for causing their mother more pain. Someone had to pull this family together, or as close together as was possible, and she wanted to be that someone. She went outside into the morning sun and sat on the top step of the porch, resting her back against the corner post of the railing. The warm sun reminded her how tired she was, her stolen corn excursion substituting for sleep. Closing her eyes, she promptly fell asleep.

Pain filled most of Mary Johnson's waking hours, either physical or mental cruelty from her father, so sleep was a balm that healed at least the surface pain. She dreamed of a large house with grass and flowers growing around a freshly painted picket fence. Her mother and father were standing in the doorway, arm in arm, waving to her as she ran down a brick walk leading to them. Mary wore a new blue dress in her dream, white lace trim accenting her new patent leather white shoes. A little white poodle jumped at her feet in excitement at her return, and she scooped the furry little creature into her arms.

Meeting at the front door, they embraced in a three way hug, the dog squirming with delight between them. Mary smiled in her sleep as she felt the warmth and love of a happy family. Her father stepped back and placed a hand on her shoulder, pride and love shining in his eyes. "Mary" he said gently.

"Yes Papa" she said dreamily, always knowing in her dreams that she could talk to him and feel no fear.

"Mary" he repeated, shaking her gently.

"Yes Papa, I'm here" she said, love filling her heart.

He placed a hand gently on each shoulder, smiled at her, and started shaking her hard. "Girl, you answer me or I'll slap you till your head rings" he roared.

Mary's eyes flew open, sleep vanishing like a thief in the night. Leaning over her, face twisted in anger and shaking her so hard her head was banging against the corner post, was her father. Terror wrapped around her like a boa constrictor crushing its victim. She tried to breathe, but fear and the drunken stench of Ray Don's breath made her gasp. Standing by his side was a man who Mary at first glance thought was a bear. He was huge, hairy, and certainly smelled as bad as a bear. The man stood with his hands shoved deep in his pockets, his shoulders sloping forward as if pointing at his huge gut. A broad grin spread his thick lips like a deep cut and his tongue flicked in and out like a snake.

Ray Don stopped shaking her and stood up, gesturing at the man bear. "Girl, I owe old Clyde here a debt which he has come to collect, and you just happen to be his payment."

Clyde laughed an oafish gawfaw and slapped Ray

Don on the back. "That's good Ray, that's real good." He leaned over Mary, still chuckling, and saliva dripped off his thick lower lip. Mary leaned to one side to avoid being dripped upon. "Little honey, you come with me and make old Clyde happy." He reached for her with a huge paw of a hand, breathing hard in anticipation.

Mary screamed as loud as she was able, surprising the two men and causing them both to back up several paces. She scrambled to her feet and leaped from the porch, pointed in the direction of the wooded area near the cabin. A hand struck her ankle, not quick enough to get a grip, but the move caused her to stumble and fall in the dust. The big man was on her in a flash, landing with a thud that seemed to shake the ground like Goliath falling from David's stone. She swung her elbow back in a tight arc, the blow landing on the big man's left temple. He grunted in pain and anger, but he rolled onto his back, stunned for a moment.

This instant was all Mary needed. She sprang to her feet and sprinted for the woods, ignoring the raging swear words coming from Ray Don. The friendly dark coolness of the pine trees swallowed her slight form like a fish going into a whale's mouth, and in an instant she was hidden from view.

A small cave covered with scrub growth was a mile into the woods, a temporary haven she found over a year ago. She ran toward its safety without hesitation, ignoring the brambles and low tree branches that scratched and tore at her skin. Running at full speed into the cave entrance, Mary skidded to a halt, almost slamming at full speed into the back wall. She quickly returned to the cave entrance, reaching out to straighten bent grass and plants, covering her entry. Moments later Ray Don came into view, cursing and breathing hard as he tried to find her. He stopped three feet from Mary's hiding place and looked about, vainly trying to find a trace of his daughter.

"Mary" he screamed, cupping his hands like a megaphone. "You come out now girl. If I have to find you

I will kill you, I swear I will." Only song birds answered. "Come take your beating and be done with it girl if you want to live, cause I swear you're dead."

Slowly, with tears streaming down her face, Mary crawled from her refuge. She stood as tall as her small frame permitted, staring defiantly at Ray Don's red face. Without a word he removed his belt and started beating her. She did not remember how long he beat her, because mercifully her mind finally took her to darkness, but at some point Ray Don threw water in her face. She was in their cabin, Clyde standing naked in front of her. Mary tried to run again but this time the big man caught her and flung her face down on the bed.

Mary braced herself for the attack, burying her face in a pillow. Feeling something small and cool pressing against her cheek, she raised her head just enough to see what it was. A shiny new dime was on the pillow.

THREE

Ray Don disappeared for nearly two months, a blessing accepted by his family with grateful relief. Martha recovered from her physical damage, but the mental anguish lingered like an open sore. Mary continued to keep her secrets to herself, fearing that she would be in some kind of trouble if anyone knew what had happened. Life had an odd way of pushing terrible events to the back of one's conscious mind, but unless it was dealt with the pain lingered.

One lazy morning the entire family, still minus Ray Don, was sitting on the porch after a hot breakfast of filling, yet boring, corn meal. The summer heat was oppressive day and night, making sleep difficult and energy levels drop. Despite the humidity, Mary felt comfortable and secure just being with people she loved. Her father almost slid from the back of her mind like a bad experience that happened long ago.

The sound of an engine and the squeak of springs as an automobile lumbered along their lane caused them to look up, more out of reflex than curiosity. A Lincoln rolled like a tank toward their front door, the shiny metal looking very much out of place as it stopped near the drab cabin. A heavily tinted windshield prevented Mary from seeing the occupants of the car, and dust settled slowly on and around the now quiet monster like a soft blanket floating slowly over a sleeping baby.

All four doors opened as if on cue, resembling an airplane with its flaps extended to lessen its speed. A severe woman dressed in a light brown business suit stepped from the front passenger side. Her hair was pulled into a bun which was so tight her eyes pulled back like an oriental. A liberal mixture of gray added ten years to her looks, which was probably early fifties. She was fit and yet matronly, with thick ankles and broad hips. She waved a flowered handkerchief in front of her face as if trying to mask a bad smell. Mary thought she looked like someone's wealthy grandmother.

A man in a dark blue suit climbed out of the driver's side of the Lincoln. He was fat and bald, the only hair visible being eyebrows and a poorly trimmed mustache. Perspiration ran from his face in tiny rivers running like tributaries through the fat folds in his face.

From the rear of the Lincoln came Rod Travers, the county sheriff. Mary's heart leaped into her throat when she saw him, wondering if he knew what his brother had done to her mother. Maybe he was here to tell them Ray Don was in jail, or even worse. She felt hope, then immediately shame for wishing bad things for her father. Sheriff Travers was a huge man, slabs of muscle straining the seams of his shirt with a waist so small he looked like an hour glass. He wore a uniform with a large tin star on the shirt pocket, and Mary could hear the leather of his utility belt creak as he stood up. The sheriff wore a campaign hat and mirrored sunglasses, seemingly required items for southern police officers.

The trio walked to the edge of the porch but only Rod Travers put a spit shined steel toed boot on the first step. The two officials hung slightly back as if touching any part of the cabin would soil them. Travers touched his hat with his thumb and index finger and nodded, the movement changing the image on his sunglasses. "Martha" he said in a deep rumbling voice.

"Sheriff Rod" she answered with a smile. "You must be hot after your long drive out here. Could I offer you some lemonade."

Mary looked at her mother in puzzlement. They

not only didn't have lemonade now, she didn't know if they ever had lemonade. There had not even been sugar in the cabin for months, but her mother looked as cool as ice as she waited for an answer.

The sheriff pulled a dingy, frayed Hav a Hank from his right pocket and mopped a bead of sweat from his forehead like a nurse sponging the forehead of a surgeon. He gave Martha a sad smile and slowly shook his head. "Thank you but no Martha, although I appreciate the offer. I'm here on official business, and sad business at that. Can I talk to you alone for a moment?"

She raised an eyebrow and pursed her lips in thought before answering. "I would imagine that any news you have for me will affect my children Sheriff, so I imagine you can just say what you have to say in front of them."

Sheriff Travers looked over the porch railing and seemed to be engrossed in watching two blue jays fighting near the tree line. They screeched noisily as they tumbled in the dust fighting for dominance. Traverse noted it was a male and a female, and also saw a scrawny cat stalking the birds. The cat was black except for a star shaped white patch on its breast. The birds were too involved in their argument to notice the predator, and Travers watched as the cat made its move, trapping the female jay with its paws.

The male blue jay went wild, pecking and flapping at the cat while screeching in ear splitting tones. Quickly the feline broke the neck of the female bird and then turned on its mate, who flew for its life into a tall tree and screeched mightily in its grief. The cat trotted away with its prize, head held high as if showing off the star in its chest.

Rod Travers unconsciously placed his hand over the badge on his shirt and turned his gaze back to Martha. He looked tired, his broad shoulders sagging under the weight of his authority. "Martha, I would suggest we talk alone. Please?" he added.

She shook her head again. "No, I believe you will

have to say it to us all."

He sighed in resignation and pulled a folded document from his shirt pocket. "Fine, we'll do it your way. Martha, I have a court order here granting custody of your children to your husband, Ray Don Johnson. The order also states that I am to escort you from these premises, take you to the county line, and tell you that if you enter the county again you will be jailed and tried for adultery and endangering children." The sheriff returned the document to his pocket and gestured toward the cabin. "You can go gather your things first if you'd like."

Martha turned a pasty white, then gray. She looked in disbelief at the sheriff, then to her children who were still as death. Mary reacted first by running to her mother and wrapping her arms around her waist in a death lock. Her lips curled back in an animal like snarl aimed at the sheriff.

"I told you we should have done this in private" he said calmly, automatically touching the butt of his pistol as he watched Mary.

"You can't take my Mama" Mary rumbled, flecks of white foam spraying from her lips as she spoke. "I won't let you take her, I swear."

The Lincoln rocked slightly as its fourth occupant emerged. Ray Don moved slowly forward, dressed in new Levi's and a fresh, clean undershirt. Jeff, Ron and Matt shrank backward, and Mary flinched but stood her ground. Ray Don stopped beside the sheriff, mumbled something to him, accepted a nod from Rod Travers, and approached his daughter.

He dropped to one knee, a friendly warm smile on his face, and placed a hand on Mary's shoulder. He squeezed with his thumb and middle finger only, appearing to just have his hand resting casually on Mary's arm. Without changing expression and barely moving his lips, Ray Don whispered, "If you give me trouble girl, first your Mama dies, then you die, and I mean nice and slow. Do you get my meanin'?"

Mary nodded, her mind draped in fear. She could not allow her mother to be hurt because of something she did. Slowly she released her hold and dropped her arms to her sides.

The pressure left her shoulder and Ray Don patted her arm. "That's better Mary, we'll get along just fine now." He stood and sauntered over to one corner of the porch, leaning against the cabin and watching and his children with a critical gaze.

Martha moved like a sleepwalker into the cabin, emerging shortly with a small carpet bag containing her possessions. She looked imploringly at the sheriff for a long moment and then walked slowly toward the car. The fat county official followed her, disappearing into the Lincoln after her as if in pursuit.

The stern woman stepped forward and addressed the children. "My name is Mrs. Merryweather and I represent county social services. We had reports that your mother was," she paused, searching for the appropriate way to say it, then said, "entertaining gentlemen. This of course will not be tolerated and we are putting a stop to this. However, I still am not so convinced we have all the details of your situation." She turned an icy glare toward Ray Don before continuing. "I will be personally checking on your welfare on a regular basis, and I assure you I am most interested in your progression."

Ray Don winked at her and waved. "I do believe you'll find we welcome you to visit us at any time Miss Merryweather" he said sarcastically.

"That's Mrs. Merryweather" was her crisp reply. "Count on my company Mr. Johnson."

"Oh, yes, yes. Mrs. Merryweather" Ray Don said, a smile playing at the corners of his mouth. "Of course you can see why I got that wrong" he sneered.

"Ray Don" the sheriff inserted with a tone of caution, "I might remind you that Mrs. Merryweather is married to Senator Charles Merryweather, and when she tells you she's going to do something I believe you can count on it."

Ray Don's smile faded and he replaced the expression with a surly frown. The sheriff turned and walked back to the Lincoln, and after another glare Mrs. Merryweather followed him. No one moved until the big car turned around, reinserted its wheels into the ruts like a locomotive on its tracks, and disappeared from sight.

Mary turned to her father, ready to die if necessary, and looked directly into his eyes. "Papa, I won't do what you made me do any more. I'll run away first, I swear I will."

Ray Don pushed away from the wall and took a step toward her, then paused as if he could hear Mrs. Merryweather's voice. He moved back to his original spot and crossed his arms in front of his chest. His easy smile caused Mary to shiver but she stood firm in her resolve. "Relax girl, nobody's going to bother you. If that county woman is going to nose around here I guess my friends won't want to come callin' anyway." He walked to his chair on the porch and dropped heavily onto its seat. "Now you go on in the house and git me my jug. It's been a long day."

Mary went obediently inside, her heart aching for her mother. She would grow, and when she was bigger and older she would find her mama. When she lifted the jug from the dirt floor in the kitchen she spied an old Barlow pocket knife her mother used to cut corn cobs in pieces for stove tinder. Quickly Mary slipped the knife into the pocket of her jeans and carried the jug to Ray Don. He took it without comment or notice of her and immediately removed the cork for a drink. Mary walked slowly from the porch and felt the knife in her pocket. She would make use of it if anyone tried to touch her again. Mary Johnson was angry.

FOUR

The next four years were surprisingly free of physical abuse as Mrs. Merryweather, true to her word, visited the children at least once each month. She took a special interest in Mary, perhaps because she was the youngest and seemed to hold the most promise of being able to break the chain of ignorance and poverty. Mrs. Merryweather felt that the story told by Ray Don was a lie, but Mary steadfastly refused to discuss what had really happened.

Rumors had run rife in the community about activities in the Johnson home, and someone had warned Ray Don that welfare authorities were discussing an investigation. He then immediately went to court with the claim that his wife had been prostituting behind his back. In the nineteen twenties this was all that was needed to condemn a woman accused of immoral acts, especially in the South. Because Ray Don Johnson was so obviously a lowlife character, at least in the opinion of Alice Merryweather, she refused to accept his story. The decision, however, was made by the judge, a long time customer of Ray Don's still, and the matter was resolved.

Mary liked Mrs. Merryweather. She was smart and sophisticated, and yet never talked down to Mary or treated her like trash as did some of the other people in town. She was always dressed well and wore the most delicious smelling perfume. Ray Don was afraid of her, which made Mary like her even more, and he usually disappeared when she came for a visit. On one such day, Mary gathered up her courage to ask a question.

"Where is my mother" she asked bluntly.

Mrs. Merryweather looked at her in surprise, as if she thought Mary should know. "I'm afraid I have no idea where your mother lives my dear. Hasn't she contacted you since she's been gone?"

"The sheriff made it real clear that she needed to get out of the county and stay out" Mary replied. "Folks like us learn that a good way to end up on a chain gang is to not do what the law says. My Mama loves us kids but she's not a fool."

"You believe your mother cares about you and your brothers?" Mrs. Merryweather asked.

"Of course she does" Mary said defensively. "Why would you ask me that?"

Mrs. Merryweather paused for a moment to carefully select her words. She put her hand gently on Mary's arm to emphasize her kindly intention before speaking. "I don't mean to be unkind dear, but your mother was, well, doing things which are not appropriate."

Mary defensively touched the Barlow knife in her pocket, a constant companion since she picked it up over four years ago. "What if Mama didn't have a choice" she glowered, anger bubbling near the surface.

Mrs. Merryweather sat straighter in her chair, one eyebrow arched in question. "Mary, I believe we always have choices concerning our behavior. Are you telling me your mother had to entertain men?"

She almost blurted out the truth, but Ray Don's hate filled eyes and his promises of death filled her mind. She remembered her mother's battered face and bit the words off before they could emerge. "I'm not telling you anything" she said and dropped her gaze.

"How long have you carried a pocket knife" Mrs. Merryweather pressed. "Usually it's the boys who carry a folding knife, not you young girls."

Mary's hand covered the bulge in her pocket like a mother bird protecting her young. She looked into Mrs.

Merryweather's eyes and did not see anger, so she relaxed just a small amount. "What makes you think I've got a knife Mrs. Merryweather?"

"Because my dear, a pocket knife leaves a very distinctive bulge in one's pocket, and besides in my line of work I've seen the business end of those things many times. Do you carry it to cut string or for protection."

"To cut string" Mary answered without hesitation.

"I see. Mary, do you feel safe here with your father and brothers?"

Mary chewed on her lower lip, trying to decide the safest way to answer the question. Finally she shrugged and said, "I feel safe since I know you'll come around on a regular basis."

Mrs. Merryweather sighed and gave her a sad smile. "Well, I need to talk to you about that Dear. My husband has accepted the position of ambassador to India. We'll be moving there next month."

Fear leaped into Mary, a glowing ember that had been waiting for the right moment to burst into flame, and she felt the weakness which accompanied its effect. "You can't go Mrs. Merryweather" she gasped. "If you go then he'll be able to... I mean Papa can....." She burst into tears.

"Oh Mary" Mrs. Merryweather said and pulled her into her arms, "what has happened to you here. If you'll tell me I can help you, I promise I will."

Mary pulled away, already forcing back the tears and pulling an indivisible hard shell around herself. "You can't help me" she said in a dull voice. "You're going away and you won't even think about me when you're in India."

"Well, you're wrong Mary. I'm giving all my files to my replacement who will come visit in my place. You will be protected from harm by her as well as me."

"Thank you Mrs. Merryweather" Mary said in a polite and formal tone. "I wish you the best in India. Please be happy there."

"Thank you Mary" she said, wiping a tear from her

cheek. "I will see you again when we're back in the States."

Mary never heard from Mrs. Merryweather again. A Miss Farnsworth dropped by one time, obviously frightened by Ray Don, who used his best backwoods attitude to show her he was in command. She instructed him in a small, timid voice to report in to her office at least once each month and fled to her compact car as quickly as possible. Mary caught her eye as she backed around to drive away, and Miss Farnsworth quickly averted her eyes in shame.

"Well now" Ray Don snarled at his children as the dust settled back on the rutted lane, "I guess your old high and mighty Merry what's her name has run out on you, jest like your mama." He spat toward the sound of Miss Farnsworth's car as it reached the hard road and sped away. "It's been awhile, but now I'm back in charge around here and it's time you ungrateful snots woke up."

Mary reached into her pocket and curled her fingers around the Barlow, determined to protect herself from her father's advances. Glancing at her brothers she saw no help there, the three boys hanging their heads in submission. Ray Don glared at Mary, rage changing to surprise as she met his eyes and did not flinch. Four years had added not only age but resolve to her twelve year old spirit.

"Don't you git started with me girl" Ray Don growled, then turned and walked toward the highway. "I'll be back around dark" he shouted over his shoulder, "and I expect all of you to be here when I get home." He was soon out of sight.

Jeff grabbed his sister's hand and pulled her toward the woods. "Come on Mary, I've got to talk to you and I don't have much time."

They hurried toward the coolness of the tree line, hand in hand like in the days they had gone to school together as children. Ron and Matt stayed on the front steps of the cabin, so terrified of Ray Don they would obediently stay in place until he returned. Mary waited until the cabin disappeared from view before pulling her oldest brother to a halt. "What do you want that can't be told in front of the boys" she said. "Especially Matt, cause he don't know most of what goes on anyhow."

"I can't take any chances" he said urgently, looking around nervously as if he expected someone to appear from nowhere. "I was in town yesterday and picked up a copy of the newspaper from the trash can outside the diner. People read it at breakfast and then throw it away. I like to read the comics."

"I don't think we came out here to talk about the comic papers" Mary said, irritated at the time Jeff was wasting telling his story.

"Okay fine, just listen. I saw in the back section of the paper where they list the legal filings for the courthouse, that a Mrs. Martha Johnson had filed for custody rights against Raymond Donald Johnson. Mary, Mama is trying to get us to live with her."

Mary's heart pounded with excitement, her hands trembling with at the thought of living with her mother. "Then Mama didn't forget about us. Jeff, we're going to live with Mama."

Jeff flinched and looked around them. Only a black squirrel was digging for a nut, but he still put a finger to his lips. "Shush, and don't go getting all excited. Just because Mama went to a lawyer don't mean some good old boy judge won't side with Papa. I'd say it's not likely anything will come of it, but at least she's trying."

"Mama" Mary whispered wistfully. Just hearing she was trying, that alone took a huge weight from her heart.

"I got something else to tell you" Jeff said nervously, digging his toe into the soft pine needle carpet of the forest floor. "I'm leaving."

Mary looked at him like she'd been slapped. Her mouth opened, snapped shut, then opened again. Finally she found her voice and said, "You're going to leave us Jeff? You're going to leave us to Papa all by ourselves?"

"Come on Mary" he begged. "I never helped with Papa anyhow, besides I'm scared half to death of him and he knows it. I didn't even have the nerve to do anything when he, well, when he hurt you." Jeff's cheeks turned crimson and he hung his head.

"You, you know what Papa did?" Mary gasped, feeling faint as she looked at his face. "I never told anyone, I never said..."

Tears began rolling down Jeff's face. He put a hand over his mouth so his next words were muffled. "I was hiding in the woods and saw him beat up on Mama. I wanted to grab a club and kill him for that, but I was too scared Mary. Then, when I saw him take you into the house," he paused and then turned so Mary couldn't see his face, "I went around to the side of the cabin and looked in the window. I saw," his voice choked off as he sobbed, "I saw what he did to you, and I couldn't stop him. I'm so sorry Mary, I just couldn't stop him."

Mary felt dead inside, a terrible sickness washing over her like a flu. She thought in an almost distracted way how odd it was that she felt shame because Jeff had seen the attack and not anger that he did not help her. Slowly she raised a hand and touched his shoulder. He flinched like her palm was a hot stove lid, and she dropped her arm back to her side. Shame turned to pity, because Mary realized despite her tender years that her brother would carry some heavy burdens with him for the rest of his life. She wanted to comfort him, to ease the pain that should never have been created in the first place. This was a problem which children were not meant to have, certainly they were not equipped to deal with such a memory.

"When I saw you in the woods that night, you didn't let on at all that you knew" she said.

"I know, I was so ashamed I thought I'd die" he said softly. "I should have charged in and killed him for what he did to Mama, and then you. I just couldn't find the courage Mary, I wasn't brave enough." He sank to the ground and covered his face with his hands.

Mary reached down and stroked her brother's hair, searching for the right thing to say. "It wasn't your fault Jeff. If Papa hadn't been doing the bad things you wouldn't have been in a position to see anything or to feel like you should have helped. Don't take fault on yourself for someone else's sin."

Jeff nodded but still covered his face. Mary sat down with her back to his and they leaned on one another, back to back with their knees pulled up. "Thank you for not hating me Sis, I don't think I could have lived with that."

"Why did you tell me?" Mary inquired. "After all, there isn't anything to be done now."

"Guilt" he simply answered. "I needed to tell you for my own attempt at peace of mind, like I deserve any."

She pushed a bit harder against his back to chastise him. "Of course you deserve peace of mind you silly. You're my brother and that's always going to be important to me." Mary sat up straighter, suddenly remembering that he was leaving. "Where are you going Jeff?"

"I don't want to tell you" he said.

"Why on earth would you not tell?"

"Because Papa would find a way to make you tell, and I'm not going to look over my shoulder all the time wondering when he's going to come out of the shadows. I'll write to you from time to time but I'll send it general delivery to the mercantile store in town. Check with them occasionally."

"When are you leaving" she asked, the ache in her heart starting already.

Jeff scrambled to his feet, offered her his hand, and pulled his sister to her feet. He put his hands, still wet from his tears, on each side of her face. "I'm leaving now Mary, before Papa comes home. If he comes late I may be a good distance away from here, especially if I can catch a ride. I figure he won't look too hard since he doesn't really care anyhow."

She pulled him to her and kissed him gently on both cheeks, tasting the salt of his tears. "Go in peace and with my love Jeff, and be happy." He pulled away and started through the woods. "And Jeff" she called out, and he paused, looking back at her. "Promise me that when you have your own family you'll treat them well and won't do like Papa."

"I promise Mary" he said softly, and melted into the trees.

FIVE

A late model Chevrolet roared over the rutted lane, bouncing erratically as it alternated between slamming its undercarriage on the hard ground and nearly becoming airborne. Mary watched open mouthed in wonder as it skidded to a halt, nearly rolling over as it tipped precariously on two wheels before drooping with a thud to the ground. Springs groaned in protest and the Chevy bounced up and down several times like a boxer balanced on his toes before it settled to a halt. The engine ticked even after the ignition was switched off, heat shimmering over the hood as a result of abuse and overwork.

Ray Don jumped from the front seat of the car and sprinted into the house, ignoring Mary, Ron and Matt. Mary followed him into the cabin and found him throwing clothes into a battered suitcase. He glanced at her and continued pulling shoes, shirts, and other personal items from a small closet. "Girl, you git into your room and grab what you want to take, 'cause we're leavin' in five minutes. Tell your brothers to move or I'll kick them somewhere into next Sunday. Now move!" he roared and Mary ran from the room.

She saw Ron and Matt disappearing into the trees as she hurried outside and knew they would not come back to the cabin until their father was gone. She ran back inside and gathered her few meager possessions, rolling them into a bundle and tying a string around it. Ray Don hurried from the cabin and threw his suitcase into the Chevrolet's back seat. He waved at her to get in the car and she scrambled into the front seat.

"Where are your brothers" he growled as he leaped behind the wheel, starting the car's engine and racing the engine to dangerous levels.

"I don't know Papa" Mary answered. I haven't seen Jeff, and Matt and Ron ran into the woods."

Ray Don looked thoughtful for a moment and then slowly grinned. He pulled the car's gear shift into first and floored the accelerator as he popped the clutch. The car threw a huge cloud of dust and pebbles into the air as the tires spun on the dirt lane. Mary grabbed the cloth seat cover as she was tossed toward the ceiling and then banged down hard when the Chevrolet leaped into the deep ruts and headed for the highway. Without pause Ray Don turned hard and burst onto the blacktop surface of the road, barely missing another car as it passed inches in front of them.

Mary watched as the outside scenery whisked by in a frightening blur, the engine roaring as her father shifted into high gear. "Where are we going" she managed to say, fear causing her to feel faint.

"Your Mama has the law after me little Sis" Ray Don said, his face a mask of hate. "She got some bleeding heart judge to say you kids can live with her, only I ain't going to have any of that. You're staying with me and that's the end of that, so's we're heading for Kentucky and we'll just see if they can find us there."

Her mouth formed a circle of surprise but no sound escaped. She swallowed hard and said, "What about the boys?"

"She can have them no good for nothin's" Ray Don growled, peering over the steering wheel. "Maybe that will keep her off my back about you."

"But I want to live with Mama" she wailed.

He flung a back hand at her face which landed on her forehead. The blow stunned her for an instant and she blinked her eyes in an attempt to clear her head. "You'll live where I say you'll live girl or I'll bust your head open" he sneered. "You shut your trap while I try to think."

Mary fell silent, her mind racing to take in what had happened. Jeff had run away to who knew where, and she was being taken to a place where she couldn't try to find his letters when she sent them. Ron and Matt had the good sense to run, so they would end up with Mama, while she would be by herself with this monster. Mary considered jumping from the car, but the speed was so great that she certainly would be killed. For the moment, she saw no choice but to comply.

Scenery flew by at a blur, the Chevrolet proving its reputation as a work horse by taking Ray Don's abuse without malfunction. They stopped at a diner in Crossville where she realized how hungry she was for real food. The wonderful smells flowing from the open windows attacked her senses with no mercy, fresh bread and hot meat loaf mixing with the scent of hot apple pie taking her breath away. Mary had eaten only corn and a few vegetables from the garden in over a month, her control almost torn from her as they entered the tiny restaurant.

"Order what you like" Ray Don said, casually pulling a wad of bills from his jeans and waving them under her nose.

"Papa, where did you get all that money" Mary gasped, "and where did that car come from" she added.

"I finally hit some ponies instead of losin' every time girl, and the car, well, I borrowed it." Ray Don leered at her with a sly smile.

Mary could not have cared less at that moment if the money had come from Satan himself, she just wanted food. A young waitress came to their table, totally disinterested in them until Mary ordered two complete dinners and a piece of pie. The waitress looked over the top of her half glasses for a moment at the tiny girl and appeared ready to comment when Ray Don spoke.

"What's the problem sweet thing, didn't you get my little girl's order?" he asked, a small grin playing around his mouth.

The waitress blinked twice and pulled her attention to Ray Don's face. "Oh, I'm sorry sir" she blustered. "I just was surprised that a little girl like that could eat so much."

"She does have an appetite" he said and pulled the thick wad of bills from his pocket. "If you're afraid we can't pay, well let me put your little mind at rest."

The girl stared open mouthed at the money, lifted her hands to her uniform top to open another button, then leaned over the table for a closer look at the money. She took her time, which in turn gave Ray Don ample opportunity to stare in return. "Wow, I guess you do have enough money to pay for the food" she said. "I wouldn't be surprised if you had enough to buy this whole joint if you'd a mind."

Ray Don casually tossed the money on the table and winked at the girl. She was trim and pretty, in her late twenties with blonde hair except for a full inch of brown growing from her scalp. A small rose was tattooed just above her left breast, peering out from the loose uniform top. Her nostrils flared slightly as if she were trying to get a scent from the money. "Say honey" Ray Don said, talking to her but not moving his eyes from the rose, "how would you like to go on to Kentucky with me and my kid here." He gestured toward Mary with one hand.

She smiled at Ray Don's forehead and leaned over just a bit farther, now eliminating all imagination from his mind. "I sure would be interested, but I have a fifteen year old boy at home. How would you feel about the two of us coming along."

A man sitting at the next table was also staring down the front of the girl's uniform, ignoring the plate of greasy potatoes sitting in front of him. He held a bottle of ketchup upside down over the plate and the condiment poured slowly like thick red blood an inch thick on top of the potatoes, finally running over the edge of the plate as he held his undivided attention on the waitress.

Ray Don glanced over at the open mouthed man and smiled at his new friend. "Excuse me for just a minute Honey" he said and slid his chair away from the table. He moved to the man's table with two fluid strides, covering the space so quickly he appeared to be floating.

The startled diner looked away from the waitress with a jerk that seemed to physically pry his eyes away from the girl. He looked up dumbly as Ray Don gently removed the ketchup bottle from his hand and noticed, again in surprise, the pile of red on his plate. His brow furrowed in confusion and he looked up in confusion just as Ray Don brought the glass bottle down on his left cheek like a batter hitting a baseball. The word Heinz leaped into his peripheral vision and grew to abnormal size as it slammed into his face. The bottle broke like a jagged knife, and the down stroke of Ray Don's swing cutting his cheek through to his gums and splitting his face to his lips, laying the flesh open like a gutted fish.

The neck of the bottle, sporting the label Served in America's Finer Restaurants, remained in Ray Dan's fist, the uneven break leaving a long, slender piece of glass resembling an icicle hanging three inches down from the A on the label. Ray Don smiled at him as the man's eyes glazed over and blood poured from his destroyed face. "You don't want to be staring at the woman I love you dumb hick" he crooned. "Maybe next time you'll show a bit of respect to a lady."

The man moaned a low, painful sound, frozen in place as if remaining motionless would make the pain subside. He looked straight ahead at nothing, his eyes blank.

"Come on girls" Ray Don said cheerfully, heading for the exit. He waved at them and walked through the open front door.

The woman snatched the money from the table and pushed it into her bra, then grabbed Mary's hand and pulled her from the little diner, running toward the Chevrolet which was roaring to life. "Come on Squirt" she said, "I don't think your old man is someone who likes to be kept waiting.

Mary was numb from witnessing the carnage and from fear, so she jumped into the back seat of the car and curled up in a tight ball on the seat. Despair flooded her heart as she realized that there was no hope for escape and her father was truly capable of anything. Each second that ticked away sped the stolen automobile further from her mother and any hope of finding her again. Sleep stole over her as a blanket of protection from the world that destroyed her spirit like a building being razed by a wrecking ball.

The car sliding to a stop in loose gravel pulled her consciousness to full alert, her muscles tensing like a jungle animal sensing a predator. They had stopped in front of a dilapidated apartment building that was probably not a fit place to live when it was built forty years ago, and now it truly appeared in danger of collapse. Paint had long since disappeared from the warped wooden frame, the building now sagging in the middle and forming a huge, lazy smile. The waitress waved to them as she ran up the broken steps, disappearing into the open doorway of the apartment building like a small fish sliding into the mouth of a whale.

Ray Don glanced over his shoulder at Mary and frowned at her as she rubbed her sleepy eyes. "This here woman has some class girl, and I don't want you doing anything to mess this up, do you understand?"

"Yes Papa" she whispered, "I won't do anything bad, but can I have something to eat?"

He looked surprised, then slapped the top of the car seat with his hand. "By criminy girl, in all the excitement we forgot to git you that food at the restaurant. If that don't beat all" he said with a chuckle. "We'll stop at a grocery and get you some lunch meat and a loaf of bread. I can't believe I clean forgot what we stopped for in the first place." He seemed in good humor and not inclined to lose his temper.

The waitress soon hurried down the steps as quickly two battered, stuffed suitcases permitted. She was followed by a boy of six feet in height with a slight but athletic build. He had shoulder length hair which was so black it looked like it was mixed with blue. A diamond chip earring gleamed in contrast in his right earlobe. His olive skin gave him a swarthy, Greek good looks, but that was marred by a scowl that appeared to be a constant companion.

The waitress flounced into the front seat of the Chevrolet, leaning over to her left to give Ray Don an open mouthed kiss like two lovers who had known each other for years. Mary flinched involuntarily when their mouths connected, then she quickly averted her eyes which fell upon the boy climbing into the back seat. He gave her a wicked grin and reached across the seat to give Mary a painful pinch on her leg. She almost yelped in pain but kept silent and only glared at the boy in anger.

The Chevrolet was soon speeding toward Interstate 71 and Ray Don whistled a tuneless song, obviously enjoying himself. He glanced at the waitress and raised an eyebrow in question. "Say Honey, I just had a thought. I don't know your name, ain't that a hoot?" He brayed like a jackass and patted the girl high on her thigh. "Actually you don't know who I am either. I'm Ray Don Johnson, and this here's my girl Mary."

The waitress patted his hand and pushed it higher on her thigh. "I'm Sharon Miller and this handsome young man in the back seat is my son Andy. He and I have been talking about getting out of that rat hole little town and you came along with a good solution." She giggled and moved closer to Ray Don. "Where we gonna go in Kentucky Sugar? I really kind of like Louisville myself, at least I always thought that would be a good place to live."

Ray Don nodded emphatically and pulled her closer. "Well now, I guess this is your lucky day Sharon honey, 'cause we're headed for none other than Louisville itself. Can you beat such a thing as that, or better yet would you want to."

She squealed with delight and nestled against Ray

Don's shoulder. "I truly am more excited than I can say. Isn't that great Andy? Imagine Louisville Kentucky." Sharon reached back and patted her son's knee, ignoring his look of distaste as the boy pulled away from her touch and shoved her hand away. "Louisville" she whispered, and planted a wet kiss on Ray Don's cheek. A pale red print of lipstick remained like a tattoo, and she rubbed it with her thumb to remove the mark.

Ray Don pulled his head from her touch, looking in the rear view mirror to see the mask. "I want to leave it" he said, "because I want to feel your kisses all the time, even after you stop."

"Oh, that's the most romantic thing anyone's ever said to me" Sharon sighed, her face flushing with delight.

"Brother, I do believe I might just throw up" Andy muttered.

The Chevrolet swung from the pavement onto a loose gravel berm and Ray Don stomped hard on the brake pedal. Mary was nearly thrown into the front seat from the force of the stop, and she saw Sharon's head thump against the windshield. Andy fell to the floor in a crumpled heap, a sharp curse escaping from him as he landed. The Chevrolet started to drift to the right, its rear end trying to catch the front, but Ray Don expertly twisted the wheel and steered the car out of its skid. The instant the Chevy came to a halt, Ray Don leaped from the car and in two strides reached the rear door. Pulling it open hard enough to damage the hinges, he reached inside and pulled a shocked Andy from the floor.

"What you doing man" Andy shouted as he exploded from the car, shock and rage mingling to give his face a look of cartoon proportions.

Ray Don hit the left side of Andy's face with an open palm, the sharp crack mimicking the report of a .22 rifle. After swinging through the strike like a tennis pro following through a shot, Ray Don backhanded the boy on his right cheek. Repeating with piston like motion, the steady crack, crack, crack of hand against face filled the humid air with unnatural sound.

Andy's eyes began to roll backward as his head snapped back and forth with the blows, until suddenly his knee jerked up between Ray Don's legs with brutal force. This would have ended the attack except his aim was slightly off center and his knee struck high on the inside of Ray Don's leg, guaranteeing a painful bruise but not causing the debilitating pain he had intended.

Only a grunt escaped through Ray Don's pursed lips as he absorbed Andy's blow, although he did pause for a moment to look at the boy's face which had turned to the color of cooked beets. Changing his open palm to a fist, Ray Don began pounding the boy's face like a one armed boxer working a heavy bag. Andy's head snapped back with each blow like a Pez candy dispenser offering a treat, until at last he went limp and Ray Don stopped his beating.

Mary heard a siren wailing from somewhere far away, the noise slowly pulling itself into her brain through the canal of her ears. She realized the sound was not the police but instead a long, thin scream coming from the front seat of the Chevrolet. Sharon's face was frozen in horror, her mouth open and her chin upturned in the same fashion as a howling dig. She reached across the bench seat of the car in a helpless gesture to reach her now unconscious son. A gurgle escaped from her throat as Ray Don threw the boy on the back seat and slammed the car door.

Climbing behind the steering wheel, Ray Don was panting from the exertion and flexing his stinging hand. He glanced at Sharon as she continued to scream and reached for her throat with his right hand. His hand closed like a mechanical vise and her scream instantly stopped. Sharon looked puzzled, her face showing an expression of curiosity and surprise. Slowly she reddened, then a blotchy purple replaced that hue. Her tongue pushed forward and past her parted lips like a snake slithering out of a dark cave, and her pretty eyes took on a dull, lifeless look that appeared as an almost invisible fog on her irises.

Very carefully and gently Mary touched her father's shoulder, feeling his muscles tremble as he applied pressure to Sharon's throat. He stared straight ahead, not looking at Sharon's distended tongue dripping saliva on his wrist, his mind appearing to be many miles away in some distant place. "Papa" she whispered in his ear, knowing full well that if she were not cautious his anger would turn to her. "Sharon will die if you don't let go of her throat. She may be dead now Papa."

Ray Don jerked his hand away as if Sharon's throat had become white hot and blistered his fingers. She dropped like a stone onto the car seat, disappearing from Mary's sight. Ray Don blinked several times and looked at Mary through the Chevy's rear view mirror. She could tell his eyes were not quite in focus and his eyebrows were knitted in a combination of anger and confusion. "What do you want girl?" he asked lazily, like a person who was waking up from a nap in the shade.

"Nothing Papa" she whispered, rubbing her fingers on the back of his neck. "I just wanted to give you a little neck rub, you know, to make you feel better. Just relax a minute Papa" she breathed, speaking slowly and carefully. She remembered a fight her father once had at the county fair with three men from Nashville. They were drunk and looking for trouble, but not anxious to tangle with too much in the way of an opponent. Ray Don was small enough to boost their confidence as they all had him by at least three inches and twenty pounds. Four men in the crowd that gathered to watch the fight pulled Ray Don off the last man or he would have surely killed him. The first two dropped like a stone and only fueled his rage. The third man was in the hospital for a month and never was quite the same, and his attempt to have charges filed was rejected because he and his friends outnumbered Ray Don and they started the fight. The same confused look was in her father's eyes when the crowd subdued him after the fight, and Mary recognized the potential for another eruption.

"What happened?" he asked with an almost childlike innocence, looking at the crumpled woman beside him.

"You were choking Sharon Papa" she whispered, still rubbing tight muscles in his neck.

"Is she dead?" he asked, not concerned but curious.

"I don't know Papa. Do you want me to see to her?" Mary asked, suppressing the urge to bolt into the front seat and administer to the stricken girl.

Ray Don rolled his head like a fighter coming back after a knockout, his eyes slowly coming to focus and his breathing coming to normal. Many remembered seeing a National Geographic special that featured mountain goats bashing their heads together in a fight over territory. The winner ended the battle in almost as poor condition as the loser, and both animals roller their necks until their heads cleared, just as her father was doing.

"Yea, why don't you see to her Girl. I'm going to get some miles behind us, but you see to Sharon for me." He started the car and pulled onto the highway with no further comment.

Mary touched Sharon's neck with her hand and felt the steady thumping of her heart. The touch caused Sharon to gasp and sit upright, then scramble over the seat into the back. Ray Don ignored her action and drove along whistling tunelessly. Sharon pulled her son into her arms and wept silently as she wiped blood from Andy's swollen face. No one spoke as the miles flew like birds heading south.

Ray Don drove without pause until he stopped at a Marathon station in Louisville. He filled the Chevrolet's tank and went inside to pay. Andy was awake and gingerly touching his face, examining his closed left eye in the rear view mirror. Sharon looked at Mary with large, doe eyes filled with fear. Mary stared back at her, not knowing what to say.

"What have I gotten my boy and me into little girl" she mumbled more to herself than to Mary.

Mary didn't answer, simply letting her face tell the frightening story. She would have stopped this nightmare herself if she knew how, but all she could really do was endure and survive.

Ray Don came back to the car carrying a bag of food purchased from the gas station market. He tossed a ham sandwich wrapped in wax paper to Mary, which she bolted down like a starving dog. He threw her a second sandwich which disappeared almost as fast as the first. Placing the bag on the front seat beside him, Ray Don turned to face the three back seat passengers. He placed his forearms on the top of the seat and pulled his legs under him, sitting back on his heels. A smile played at the corners of his mouth, making him appear playful except for the glint of madness in his eyes.

"I got something to say and I don't want to have to repeat this" he said, still playing the roll of friend and confidant. "I want Sharon to be respected by all of you. I don't care if it's a relative or a stranger, no one will give this woman any grief when I'm around." Ray Don's eyes blazed in emphases, and a bead of sweat popped out on his upper lip.

He turned his eyes to Sharon, a steel cold look which caused her to pull back even further into the seat cushions. "If I discipline one of the children, your mouth stays shut or I will shut it for you. I will have no interference when I run my house, and I'll kill you if it happens again."

Sharon blinked hard to clear tears from her eyes and opened her mouth to speak. Mary reached over and squeezed her hand at which point Sharon closed her mouth with a snap. She glanced out of the window like a prisoner looking for a way to escape. Mary slid her hand away and sat as still as possible. Ray Don seemed to notice what she did but made no comment.

"Now, let's find a place to stay" Ray Don said with a broad smile. He turned around, started the Chevy with a flourish, and roared down a side street. He drove a short distance and pulled into a shabby looking trailer park, the first residences they saw. A small wooden sign with a hand lettered word, MANAGER, painted in faded white paint was staked at a twenty degree list in front of a dirty mobile home. A car port sagging in the middle to the point of collapse hung inches from the top of a rusted Yugo. Yellow curtains that once were white hung in shreds like a beleaguered battle flag, hiding next to nothing inside the metal frame home.

A tall, slender man with hunched shoulders and a full face white beard moved snail like onto a chipped cement form landing. He first appeared to have chocolate melted in the hair around his mouth, but he seemed to want to prove this wrong by spitting a long stream of tobacco juice in the general direction of his small patch of weed infected grass trying vainly to grow beside his home. Ben Franklin glasses perched on the end of his nose and he tilted his head down to peer over them with rheumy eyes at his visitors. Remnants of his tobacco juice hung suspended from his beard, then disappeared inside like a sponge picking up a spill.

"Good evening sir" Ray Don said in his most charming voice. "Do you have any homes for rent by the day or even perhaps by the week. My family and I are settling down here and need a nice place to live while we put down our roots."

The old man squinted and then snorted out something like a laugh. He scratched an armpit through a short sleeve work shirt stained white with sweat and then sniffed his fingers with a look that seemed somewhat like satisfaction before answering, "Well, I got some places to rent if you don't mind living with colored's. We're about half and half here. Rent's in advance and utilities are included unless you run water all day and night and start leavin' night lights on and the like. In that case you can pay more or out you go."

"We're quiet and not much for the night life" Ray

Don said, "so I don't imagine you'll find us much of a problem. We just want a quiet place you know, and the coloreds don't bother me if they live like good neighbors."

"Well, I reason you can try it for a spell" the old man said, waving an arm toward the rear of the court. "You'll see a gray unit marked number sixty six near the end of this street. If you want it come on back up here and pay me for two weeks in advance. The rate is posted on the front door. If you move out sooner I'll just refund you."

"Fine" said Ray Don. "How do we get in?"

"The key's in the door" the manager said. "If you're not going to stay, just leave everything the way you find it."

Ray Don waved and slid into the Chevy, a big grin on his face. "Well, we got a place to stay. You three can unload while I go back and pay the old buzzard."

The car's headlights played on a variety of ill kept trailers with sagging clothes lines and cars resting on cement blocks like false god's on a throne. Number sixty six was a two bedroom with the shell of what once was a Florida room which now had faded green plastic grass carpeting and the skeleton of a frame as the only proof of its prior existence. The front door was warped and at first Mary was convinced her father could not force it open, but after a stream of swear words it burst open when he pushed his shoulder against the jamb.

Mary turned a wall switch just inside the door and a bug filled globe hanging in the kitchen and covering a forty watt bulb came to life. Tiny scuttling noises on the kitchen linoleum brought their eyes down to dozens of roaches scurrying for cracks in the baseboard and the cover of darkness. A discolored faucet dripped rusty water into a porcelain sink that was scratched and chipped to the point of exposing more cast iron than white surface. Dust and dirt were everywhere, and just walking on the threadbare living room carpeting caused tiny poufs of dust to rise into the air.

Her stomach turned when she turned on the light in

the small bathroom, revealing a tub almost black with mold and soap scum and a toilet almost filled to the rim with waste so old it had a crust on its surface. Backing into the hall with bile rising into her throat, Mary moved on to the two bedrooms. Neither bed had headboards, just a springs and mattress resting on a metal frame. Stains covered the mattress like a Palomino and lumps rose up like growths on a deformed person's back. She was convinced they would not stay in this horrid place.

She found Sharon and Andy carrying their belongings into the trailer from the car. "What are you doing? Surely we're not going to stay here" she protested.

"Your father walked to the manager's office to pay the rent" Sharon said in a hollow voice. "He told us to bring in our things and said you should clean the bathroom."

Mary's stomach lurched again and she shook her head. "I can't do that. Did you see that toilet? I can't clean that place."

"Fine, you tell him that when he gets back" Sharon said with a shrug.

Minutes later Mary stood in the stinking bathroom with a bucket, rags, soap, and a plunger. She noticed a small sign fastened with a finishing nail hanging over the cracked mirror above the sink. Dirt covered the painted message, so Mary began her task by cleaning the wooden placard that had been purchased years before from someone at a county fair booth. Tears filled her eyes as she removed the layers of soil and revealed the message surrounded by little hearts burned into the surface of the wood. The message was 'Home Sweet Home'.

SIX

Three days were needed to transform the interior of the mobile home into a place fit for humans to dwell. Mary did all of the work, the bathroom and kitchen being the worst rooms to clean. Ray Don was gone at first light the morning after their arrival, and Sharon had not emerged from the rear bedroom. Andy was gone before dawn each day and returned long after Mary fell asleep on the living room sofa. She accepted that as her bed without discussion or comment when Andy took the second small bedroom.

When everything smelled like ammonia and Murphy's Oil Soap, she stood back and admired her work. The small trailer was old and worn but at least was fresh and clean. If the roaches stayed after their food supply was eliminated she didn't see them. Mary took great care to insure the meager supplies available were covered and sealed as tight as possible.

She wondered if Sharon might be dead in the rear bedroom and actually wished for her to come out so she could clean the room. Going to the closed door, she gingerly turned the knob. Locked. Mary pressed her ear to the thin, hollow core door and held her breath while she listened for noises. When she became light headed from oxygen deprivation Mary released her lungs and pulled in a gulp of air. She had not heard a sound from the bedroom. She raised her fist to knock on the door, hesitated, then dropped her arm. If Sharon were dead she would not respond anyway, and if she were hiding her reaction would probably be one of anger. The prudent decision was to ignore the back bedroom and go exploring.

Emerging from the tiny mobile home, the blast of

warm air and bright sunshine made her feel free and alive. Her heart raced with excitement as she skipped across the dirt path in front of the noses of the trailers and ran toward a small park with a rusted swing set and a sliding board that listed several degrees to one side. The slide was bright and shiny from countless polishing by seats of trousers and backs of dresses. The metal was hot to the touch from the sun, but an invisible film of wax deposited by children rubbing the slide with wax paper made the surface lightning fast. Mary slid down several times, leaning to her right to counteract the slide's list, and flying off the end to hit the ground running before doing an about face and sprinting for the ladder and another trip down.

She paused after one such thrill ride and stared at a girl of about her own age standing beside an oak tree which served as part of an informal fence around the playground. She was the color of dark chocolate, with coal black hair pulled severely back into two pigtails. Her dress was fashioned from a red and white checked Pillsbury flour sack, and her bare feet were covered with dust. Mary walked slowly toward the girl, each sizing the other up like two deer, wanting to be friendly but ready for flight.

Mary spoke first, smiling shyly and waving a hand like a butterfly flittering around a flower. They stopped about four feet apart, staring at one another as if looking at an image in a mirror. Curiosity pushed Mary past her shyness and helped her to speak. "Hi, I'm Mary. What's your name?"

"Myra."

"Myra" Mary echoed. "That sure is a pretty name. Would you like to play with me?"

"I sure would" Myra answered, her head bobbing enthusiastically and beating her shoulders with her pigtails. "Some white kids aren't allowed to play with me, so I thought I'd better let you ask first."

"What in the name of heaven do you mean" Mary asked, not sure if she were serious or kidding.

"Because of my skin color Silly" Myra answered. "Some white folks don't want their children playin' with us."

"Because you're black?" Mary interrupted. "That's sure enough got to be the silliest thing I ever heard."

Myra frowned and raised one eyebrow. She puffed out her cheeks in thought before making a reply. "Where are you all from?" she asked.

"Tennessee. We lived in the hills where neighbors, no matter what their color, were welcome."

"Well, you sure haven't lived around no big cities" Myra chuckled. "Ever now and then I see some kid getting his what for after getting too friendly with one of us."

"I don't think my Papa much cares what I do or who it's with" Mary said a little sadly. "Besides, I could use a friend right now."

"Then you got one Mary, Mary, whatever your last name is" Myra said with a smile.

"Johnson, Mary Johnson."

"Okay then Mary Johnson, my last name is Parker. By the way, why aren't you in school today?"

"I don't know" Mary said honestly. "I don't know anything about the schools here or where I should go. Have they started?"

"About a week ago" Myra said. She gestured in a general direction over her shoulder. "The school's over on Union Street, right near the Methodist Church. I'd bet you could walk on over there and just start if you'd a mind."

"Why aren't you in school" Mary asked.

"The black school's only open when they can find a teacher, which they don't have right now. Miss Pinkney died this Spring from influenza, and I don't guess the school board is in too big a hurry to spend money hiring a new teacher. Besides, they usually have to pay more for our school."

"Why is that, I mean a school's a school, and I don't understand how they can just shut a school because one teacher dies."

Myra giggled and ran for a turn on the slide. She climbed to the top and paused for a moment before pushing off the slippery surface. "Girl, you sure must have had a sheltered life. The black school don't have but one teacher, and white folks don't want to teach us nothin'."

"Then why not hire a black teacher" Mary asked reasonably, climbing the ladder for her turn on the slide.

"There might be some black teachers in big cities like Detroit or New York, but there sure aren't any around these parts" Myra answered as she watched her new friend flash by on the slide. "We just make due with what we got. Besides, I'd rather play than go to school anyhow."

"Well, if you're not going to go than neither am I" Mary said with determination. "You and I will just spend our days together and have fun." She went to her new friend's side and put her arm around her shoulders. "It'll just be you and me against the world Myra Parker."

"That's a bargain Mary Johnson." Myra looped her arm around Mary's waist. "Friends for life."

Mary nodded. "Friends for life."

SEVEN

The two unlikely friends became inseparable over the next weeks. Mary's only duties were cleaning the small mobile home, that task only complicated on the day after she met Myra when Sharon finally emerged from her room. The filth inside was equal to the conditions in the rest of the trailer when they moved in, and the better part of a day was needed to clean the bedroom. Minutes after she finished the task Mary went to the kitchen to clean up the mess Sharon had created after cooking half their supplies and eating them in one sitting. She brushed past Mary without a word, closed and locked the bedroom door, and stayed there for three days. She emerged only to eat and use the bathroom, then repeated the process. It seemed amazing that she could wait so long between eating and bathroom visits, and Mary finally concluded that while she was out playing with Myra, Sharon made secret trips to relieve herself and grab a snack to eat.

Ray Don must have returned from time to time as groceries appeared in boxes on the kitchen counter. Mary cared for her own needs and presumed the seldom seen Andy and Sharon were taking care of themselves. She was really very happy, using the time to play games and explore with Myra. Without realizing it she was catching up some of her missed childhood.

The trailer park was its own little world, existing without the need or interference of anyone outside the spider web of dirt roads leading to each group of trailers. Myra was a budding gossip columnist, full of information and secrets about the people who made the dreary little metal island their home. They walked slowly along, stopping at the front of this mobile or that, Myra leaning close to Mary and whispering about the occupants of each. The nose of each trailer home stuck out at them like a dog sniffing a stranger, making Mary feel nervous yet excited as she imagined being overheard by the metal creatures.

"This here is where Ester Truitt and her crazy boy lives" Myra was saying. "Ester is a white woman and for a long time lived with a black man who I never met so I don't know his name. It was the talk of this place and they were always in danger of getting run out."

"Why would they get run out?" Mary asked, trying not to stare at the closed curtains on the front window.

"Because of the mixed race marriage you ninny" Myra said with irritation. "Why do you think I have to go to another school than you for criminey sakes. We aren't supposed to mix in with one another you see, so there's big trouble."

"You said her boy is crazy. Is that because he has a white mama and a black papa?" Mary asked.

Myra laughed and playfully pushed her friend. "Of course not you silly girl. There ain't really a thing wrong with white and black folks mixin' together, it's just a stupid prejudice that dumb people have."

"It all seems strange to me" Mary mused, then she put her index finger against her nose in puzzlement. "Then why is he crazy Myra?"

Myra walked slowly away from the trailer, pulling Mary's hand to urge her along. "Did you see the curtains move a bit? Someone was watchin' us from the kitchen. Come along and I'll tell you why that boy's crazy."

Neither girl spoke again until they were out of sight of the trailer, then Myra finally looked over her shoulder and seemed to relax. "That boy is crazy" she continued, "because a mob of idiots from this trailer park decided one night that these people were going to move along. They tipped that trailer right over on its side when they yelled out the window for them to get lost 'cause they weren't comin' out. Ester's man was killed when he landed on his head and broke his neck. It must have been wild in there when that trailer went over and threw them tea kettles over elbows. Ester was holdin' the baby and he flew out of her hands like a hot potato and slammed face first onto the top of the trailer, which by that time was the side of the trailer. If you looked at that baby he seemed just fine after all that. He just laughed and cooed like the best baby. The problem is, he grew up with about half the wits he needed to be normal. Folks pretty much figure it was that shot in the face that made his brain a mess of grits."

Mary was fascinated by the story, her mouth hanging open in wonder. "What did the mob do after they killed that poor man and hurt the baby?"

"They did what all stupid morons in a group like that do" Myra said, snorting like a bull through her nose to demonstrate disgust, "they slunk away like a bunch of whipped dogs. They probably ended up in some bar and got to braggin' about it later on, liquor bringing back their courage."

Mary was sensitive enough to be stricken by the story, but had felt enough personal abuse that she was not surprised. Adults in her world more often than not were cruel and spiteful, seeming to enjoy the infliction of pain. Seeming to underscore her feelings, Mary watched a young hawk chasing a large black crow in a nearby tree. The crow cawed with fear and anger, trying to escape the knife sharp beak of the hawk. The crow flew from branch to branch in a vain attempt to escape its tormentor, but the hawk followed each movement, slashing and biting at each stop.

The chase continued for several minutes, Mary moving around on the ground to watch the drama as it unfolded. Finally the crow fell from a tall branch and dropped like a stone, landing lifeless on a soft cushion of brown pine needles on the ground. The hawk screeched a cry of triumph, shook its wings in victory, and flew away.

Mary approached the dead bird and looked at it sadly. Myra tugged at the sleeve and asked, "What are you botherin' about that old crow for Mary?"

Mary looked at her friend and wiped away a tear from the corner of her eye. "I want that poor bird to know that someone saw what happened to it and cared enough to be sad" she said. "That's more than most folks get."

Myra put her arm around Mary's shoulders, patting her gently on the back. "I'm glad to have you as my friend Mary. If you care about a bird you must really think a lot of me."

"I'd think more of you if you'd grow some feathers" Mary teased, and both girls giggled.

"Come on, I want to tell you more about this place" Myra urged, pulling her friend away from the fallen bird. "Over here lives Hazel Muirwood. She has seven kids, all one year apart, and they live in that two bedroom tin can. Can you believe that?"

"And they got a Papa living with them?" Mary inquired.

Myra laughed, a pleasant mirthful sound that was pleasant to Mary's ears. She playfully swatted Mary on the arm and bent over in exaggerated mirth. "That would be a dang good trick I want to clue you" she howled.

"And what's so funny Miss Giggles" Mary asked, laughing at herself as Myra's giggling infected her.

"Well, Hazel has never been married and takes on a different man about every other month" Myra said, regaining her composure enough to continue the story. "Chances are those seven kids all have a different daddy and there won't none of them ever know who he is."

"There seems to be about anything here except normal families" Mary reasoned.

"I imagine" Myra agreed. "Just be glad you got a mama and daddy like normal folks."

Mary frowned but didn't comment, not wanting to talk about her personal situation. She moved on, hoping

62

that Myra would quickly find another subject to gossip about. She didn't have long to wait, as Myra pulled her arm and pointed to another trailer home.

"You see that one? That's Moses Blackburn's place. He's been in prison twice for stealin' and once for forcin' himself on a woman. My mama says it's a disgrace he has a Bible name he's such a bad one, and my daddy says he just causes more trouble for us black folks. I got to tell you, he's the best lookin' man you'll ever see in these parts, and rumor has it he's been in more homes in this trailer park than you could shake a stick at. He don't work himself, so he just watches until some man goes off to work and then he knocks on the door. Often as not he's invited in and he don't come out for at least an hour. You figure out what he's doin' in there."

"I don't suppose he's just visiting" Mary said quietly, flashes of her experiences with men going through her mind.

"Yea, or selling magazine subscriptions" Myra said and giggled at her own humor. "You know, they say Moses is going to get caught sometime and get himself shot by some husband, but he don't seem to worry about that. He's really open about what he does."

The girls finished their tour of the trailer park and came back to their favorite spot, the park with the crooked slide. Plopping down on the ground, they rested their backs against a large oak tree and stared at the ramshackle trailer Mary now called home. Her thoughts drifted to her mother and brothers as they sat in silence, her heart aching as she imagined Mama hanging laundry on the clothes line, her tan skin looking beautiful in contrast to white sheets from their beds. Ron and Matt would be hauling water and chopping wood for the stove, waiting for a big pot of vegetable soup to cook for dinner. She pictured Jeff coming home, wealthy and successful from working, and bringing presents and food for the family.

"What are you smiling at" Myra asked.

Her voice brought Mary back to the present, reality pushing the pleasant fantasy from her mind. "Oh, I was just thinking about the future" she said with a dreamy smile. "Myra, what do you hope for in the future?"

"Honey, I don't even get to go to school" Myra said ruefully. "My best chance is to marry a boy who works at the mill, get some kids, and make a home."

"But don't you want more than that?" Mary asked.

"Of course I do, but I'll be lucky if I get what I just said" Myra replied. She picked up a handful of stones and threw them, one by one, at the metal ladder on the slide. Several found their mark and plinked as they hit. "I don't know if I'll end up pretty or if I'll have a good figure to attract a working man. Lots of my people can't get work, at least not if a white man wants it, and so the ones that have jobs pick the best lookin' girls."

"That's awful" Mary said.

"That's life" Myra countered.

The silence took over again until Mary said, "Let's make a pact."

"Okay" Myra agreed without knowing what the agreement even involved. "What is it?"

"Whichever one of us becomes successful, we'll find the other and share it equally. Besides, we're friends forever. We already agreed on that."

"That's a deal" Myra said with a smile. She spat on her palm and held her hand out to Mary, who spat on her own before they shook hands. "Spit sticks us together you know, like sisters" she said.

"I would be proud to call you my sister Myra Parker" Mary said.

"Right back to you Sis" Myra said with a wink. "Remember now, we can't forget this."

"Myra, there are things I will never forget" Mary said with a smile. "One day maybe I'll tell you all about it, but for now just know that I don't forget anything important, and you're important."

"You know, this is getting too serious for me" Myra said and scrambled to her feet. "Let's heat up this old slide with our back sides and see how fast we can go." She giggled as she ran for the ladder and called over her shoulder, "Last one there is an old dead dog."

Mary leaped to her feet and prepared to pursue, but she stopped in her tracks with a big smile melting from her cheeks. Their trailer home caught her eye, a beam of sunlight bouncing off the door as it swung open. A tall, well built black man was casually coming down the metal steps, his strikingly handsome face wearing a broad smile that revealed perfect white teeth. Sharon stood just inside the door, dressed in an open robe with nothing on beneath its dingy silkiness. She touched the man's arm as he stepped down and blew him a soft kiss when he looked back to her.

Myra had quietly come to Mary's side, her jaw hanging open in shock and disbelief. Both girls turned their heads as if they were connected by a metal rod, and simultaneously saw at the same time, Ray Don and seven friends he had met at the trailer park standing no more than ten feet from the stranger. They reacted rather slowly because they were drunk, but they still leaped forward as one. Sharon's eyes flew open wide in horror when she saw them and she immediately screamed "Rape!" Filling her lungs again she screeched "Rape, rape, rape, rape!"

"That's Moses Blackburn" Myra gasped, and Mary felt her heart leap to her throat.

The men fell upon Moses like wolves on a sheep, not making a sound as they began pounding and kicking at him. Mary thought it odd that she didn't think of anything, except how interesting it was that the men went about their task like laborers in a factory, just doing their job and finding no reason to comment. Sharon continued to scream, but her voice seemed to have muted and no sound came to Mary's ears.

Time stood still as the small mob continued their beating. Moses squirmed and rolled, alternately covering his head and then his stomach and groin with his arms. He pushed his face flat into the dirt to avoid getting hit in the face, but heavy boots kicked his ears until they split open and blood flowed from them like warm sap from a maple tree. An occasional crack that sounded like a branch breaking indicated bones as they broke from the onslaught. Finally he lay still as they pounded him, either from unconsciousness or total submission.

They stopped because of fatigue and the end of their adrenaline rush, not because they thought he had enough. With the completion of their work, Mary's ears turned back on and she heard Sharon's screams again, punctuated from time to time by the shrill cry of "Rape!"

Ray Don was bent over at the waist, his hands propped against his knees and smearing blood from his bruised and torn knuckles on his dirty Levi's. He pulled air into his lungs in gasps as deep as years of cigarette use would allow, his back heaving up and down with effort. Finally he stood slowly erect, moving slowly toward Sharon as she continued to scream in the doorway. He climbed two stairs with the speed of an old man, his head down on his chest as if his energy was gone.

Sharon held her arms out to him, tears pouring from her eyes like a small stream in the Spring. With lightning speed Ray Don's fist pistoned up and hit the very tip of her jaw. She fell like a marionette whose strings were just cut, unconscious before she hit the floor in a heap. The clack of her upper and lower teeth as they came together with the sound of two marbles hitting each other in a sack rang in Mary's ears a moment or two after Sharon's limp arm fell over her face. Ray Don spit through the open door and turned his attention toward Moses.

"Well boys" he roared, pushing his chest forward like a bantam rooster, "it would appear we have a couple of choices here. We either turn this low life rapist over to the law where he gets put in jail and lives a life of ease and comfort until he dies of old age, or we show him a bit of

Kentucky justice right here and now."

"I reakon we show him what happens when you mess with another man's woman" one of the men said. He pulled a pint bottle of whiskey from his back pocket, took a drink, grimaced as it jolted his system, and passed it to a man on his right. "Or better yet, let's drive him to the police station, but we don't let him ride in the car."

"He ain't ridin' in my car" Ray Don bellowed as he snatched the whiskey bottle from a weaving fat man whose belly button swelled forward like a stop sign sticking out from his undershirt.

"We can take my car" another man offered. "It's got a trailer hitch so we can tie him off on that."

A rope appeared as if out of nowhere and was tied securely to the hitch mounted on the rusted bumper of an old Pontiac. The other end of the rope was looped around Moses' legs and tied off around his neck like a noose. The mob pushed and squeezed into the car until there was no more room, then the one remaining straggler climbed on the trunk so no one was left out. Mary was convinced the man was dead as he lay on his back, arms stretched out to each side, his eyes closed to block out the reality of what was happening.

The car's engine sprang to life in a smoke belching roar, the rotted muffler doing little to silence the powerful engine. Just as the rear tires began to spin, throwing a small shower of stones and dirt into the air, Moses opened his eyes and turned his head toward the two girls. Mary locked onto his face and he reached a hand out imploringly. She saw his lips move as the rope snapped tight and his body shot forward like a stunt man rocketing from a cannon.

Myra was trembling as they watched the car speed away, the men hooting and laughing as Moses bounced and rolled behind like a rag doll tied to a string. As the car rounded a sharp bend in the road Moses swung wide like a skier on a rope. A tall maple tree stood unmoving at the edge of the road, a beacon to the battered form as it was dragged along. Moses' head slammed into the tree with the sound of a melon being thumped by a careful shopper. The girls turned their heads away and the men hooted even louder at the brutal results of the collision.

"What did he say when they started draggin' him?" Myra inquired, shock causing her facial muscles to sag and making her look old.

Mary swallowed hard and wiped her hand over her eyes. "He said over and over, 'Pray for me. Please pray for me' " she whispered.

Without speaking another word the two friends took each other by the hand, sank slowly onto their knees, bowed their heads, and prayed.

EIGHT

Mary didn't return to the trailer until after dark. She was hungry and tired, finally to the point that she cared more about food and sleep than the unpleasant home life. The front door was standing open, a small lamp in the living room spilling light out of the opening. The effect was the appearance of warmth and welcome, exactly the opposite emotions which prevailed in the home.

Spots of dried blood dotted the floor in memory of Sharon's split lip, given to her by Ray Don when he punched her earlier that day. Mary automatically thought that she must scrub the entry in the morning. She looked around the kitchen and living room, everything seeming to be in place and as she left it that morning. The quiet was deafening, leaving her with a feeling of unease which caused her to roam through the trailer home despite overwhelming fatigue.

The bathroom exploded with light as she moved the switch to the on position, exposing a dingy yet clean room, again looking very normal. Mary went to Andy's room, the bright bathroom light serving her well enough to see that the room was empty. She glanced at the open closet door and saw that it contained only several bent wire hangers.

Moving quickly to the other bedroom, she turned the knob without knocking and the door opened to another empty room. Only Ray Don's clothes were there, mostly strewn about the room in small piles. The bed was even stripped of its sheets and mattress pad, ugly yellow and brown stains and several large lumps on the mattress exposed to the world like great sores. One pink ladies slipper peeked out from between the mattress and springs, hidden safely from hurried hands that had quickly packed the few possessions.

So Sharon and Andy were gone, disappeared like two trustee convicts from a prison, escaped to freedom and hopefully a better life. Mary felt envy and even a little bit of anger that they had not taken her with them, but fatigue dragged other emotions to the background as she moved woodenly to the front room sofa. She didn't turn off the light or even close the door and was asleep the instant her head touched a cushion.

Noise slowly drifted in from far away like a coffee pot slowly beginning to perk. Mary fought the urge to awaken, her subconscious demanding more rest but losing to noises and light from the world. She sat slowly upright, her head aching from the hard sleep and her mouth dry and rancid. Sunlight fell through the open door and a mixture of automobile engines and voices were heard as the trailer park came alive for another day. Stumbling to her feet, Mary closed the door and went toward the bathroom. She felt better after a warm bath and a thorough brushing of her teeth, then hunger surfaced and pushed her to the kitchen.

Four eggs, a half pound of bacon, and three slices of bread were all that remained to eat. Soon all the food was in her, and Mary felt as good as was possible. She had just finished washing and drying the dishes when she heard the trailer door open. Ray Don came in, stumbling slightly in drunkenness, and whistling a small tune.

Mary froze in place, wondering how he might react when he discovered Sharon and Andy were gone. He winked at her and shambled toward the bedroom, bumping each side of the hallway like a pinball as he went. He didn't enter the bedroom, simply staring in as if confused at what he saw. He turned, holding the door jamb for support, and glared at his daughter.

"What's going on around here" he growled.

Mary swallowed hard and said in a small voice, "I think Sharon and Andy left us Papa. I came home last night and they were gone, and it looks like they took their clothes and everything."

Ray Don smiled and pointed an unsteady finger at her. "Well, good. She was a tramp and that boy wasn't worth a bullet in his head. I got to say, I was pretty sick of them myself."

Encouraged by his attitude, Mary returned his smile. "Well, I guess it's just you and me Papa, but I can take care of this place for you."

He stumbled forward, banging his head on the wall as he fought for balance. "Well, that's just fine with me. And do you know what else little girl?"

She dropped her guard then, thinking they would be all right for at least a while, the smile on her father's face making her forget what he was, just long enough for him to reach her. "What Papa" she answered, hungering for some parental kindness.

Ray Don put his hands on her shoulders, his smile turning hard and his eyes going dead. "Now that we're alone, I figure this is a good opportunity for us to get close again girl, you know what I mean?" His fingers closed tight, pain blossoming in her shoulders like unfolding flowers.

"No" she gasped, the pain bringing back reality to her mind. She jerked back, breaking his hold on her and sprinting to the door. He caught her as she turned the knob, the force of his pull on her shoulder shooting the door open like a cork escaping from a bottle.

Mary clawed the edge of the door as her father pulled her to him, her index and middle fingernails splintering and tearing away from her right hand. She felt her feet leave the ground and saw the world spin just as she remembered rides at the county fair, but this ride was not exciting or thrilling, it was terrifying. Breath whooshed from her body as Ray Don threw her over his shoulder like a bag of potatoes and marched into the rear bedroom.

The stained mattress rushed up to slap her face as Ray Don threw her on her stomach and planted a hand in the small of her back. A foul smell assaulted her nose as it was shoved into a yellow stain that forced bile into her throat.

When Ray Don threw her on the bed, her arms were pinned under her. Mary wiggled a hand into the pocket of her jeans, ignoring the searing pain in her fingers where the nails had been. Curling her hand into a fist, she grasped the knife that had been her constant companion for years. It felt cool and hard to her touch and gave her renewed strength to fight what was about to happen.

Throwing her over onto her back, Mary saw that her father had stripped to the waist and loosened his trousers. His eyes had that glazed look he acquired when he spun out of control, and he drooled down his chin as he pulled her jeans around her ankles. This caused her hand to fly from the pocket, the knife still clutched in her fist. It fell on the mattress as she flexed her throbbing fingers and she frantically groped about, trying desperately to retrieve her metal friend.

Ray Don made an evil, guttural sound in his throat and threw his head back like a wolf prepared to howl over a fallen sheep. He lifted his naked chest above her, his heart visibly pounding just left of center. He placed a stiff arm on the mattress beside each of her shoulders, prepared to begin his assault.

The knife seemed to find her hand, the weight of Ray Don's knees on the mattress actually causing it to slide over to her. Without an instant of thought she grabbed the handle with her palm and four fingers and slid the nail of her thumb into the long notch creased along the closed blade. She had opened the Barlow hundreds of times in the past in exactly the same way, practicing for this very moment that she had prayed would never happen. The blade swung easily from its protective cover, locking into place with a solid snap as its finely crafted mechanism worked without flaw. Ray Don heard the blade snap open and he paused for a long moment as if asking his brain to understand what his ears had heard. This pause caused him to hold steady like a target with a bulls eye painted on it, and Mary pushed her arm forward with all her strength.

When they had lived in the Tennessee cabin they would occasionally go to town. She had seen the traveling tool sharpener do tricks with knives, his entertainment drawing children and in turn their parents with shovels, hoes, axes and knives to be sharpened. He always said the most important thing to remember about knives was you are not stronger than them. Always use more force than you might feel is necessary to do the job, because the knife can take the punishment.

Mary saw the tool sharpener in her mind slamming a hunter's knife through a thick branch from a hickory tree, his face contorted with concentration and effort as the blade exploded through the rock hard wood. She imagined his strong, steady arm, corded with muscle, holding the Barlow instead of herself. She felt the point of the knife hesitate as it pressed against Ray Don's skin like a finger pressing against a balloon. When his skin yielded to the blade, it leaped forward, hungrily searching for vital organs to pierce.

One rib stood as sentinel against the attack, but the blade slid by this obstruction without pause and slanted upward slightly to overcome the problem. Mary's fist, holding tight to the handle of the knife, punched Ray Don's chest like a boxer delivering a body shot. The knife handle struck with such force that it actually penetrated slightly into the wound.

Ray Don stood straight up, the glaze over his eyes melting away and replaced by a bright shine of fear and pain. Slowly, like a giant tree grudgingly giving in to the bite of a chain saw, he fell back and crashed to the floor. His body spasmed once, than twice, and he lay still.

Pulling her pants over her naked thighs, Mary made

little mewing noises as she saw her father stretched motionless on the floor, the knife now sticking out like a flag pole. A movement in the doorway caused her to stifle a scream as she saw Myra standing there with her hands covering her mouth. Their eyes met and they ran to each other, sobbing and clinging to one another for comfort.

"Mary, I saw" Myra sobbed as she hugged her friend. "I saw him pull you from the door, and I crept down the hall to this room. I saw what he was fixin' to do and I was gonna jump on his back. Just before I moved you stuck him and he fell down here dead."

"Do you really think he's dead Myra?" Mary said, terror swelling up like a storm.

"He sure enough looks dead to me" she said. "I got to guess a knife in the chest has every right to kill someone."

Mary grabbed her friend's arm and pulled her from the room, the sight of Ray Don dead on the floor too much to take. The girls huddled in the hallway and needlessly whispered. "What am I going to do" she said, pulling at Myra's arm as if she could force a solution to tumble out.

"Well, you only were protectin' yourself" Myra said, "so there isn't no way you should feel bad about this. You just did what had to be done to stop him."

Mary nodded vigorously, her teeth chattering with fear. "So all I have to do is tell the police he was going to... you know" Mary said, "and everything will be all right."

"I didn't say that" Myra replied with a shake of her head.

"What do you mean" Mary demanded. "You saw what happened. I didn't have a choice but to stab him, you just said that."

"Will your mama and brother back you up?" asked Myra.

Mary dropped her eyes and shook her head. "That wasn't my mama or my brother. Papa picked her up at a restaurant along the way and they've been living with us.

They ran off after Papa and those men killed Moses."

Myra sighed and frowned, her large eyes looking hard into Mary's fear. "Then you're a girl with no family and you've got a dead man in the other room. What do you think the law will do about that?"

"I don't know" Mary said in despair. "What can they do? You saw what happened."

"Of course I did, but what's the easiest thing for them to do? They'll send you to the girls' reformatory because that's cheaper than the children's home. In the reformatory they don't have to feed you right or send you to school or hire social workers to help you find a new home. It's just the easiest and cheapest way to handle it Mary."

"Then what do I do" Mary said, despair crowding out thought.

"If it were me, I'd get out of here and head for another State" Myra said. "Maybe Ohio. Most folks won't think you're headed North, so that's safest. If we leave the front door open someone will come by and find the body. By the time it all gets put together you'll be long gone. I don't think the law will look too hard for the killer of someone in this trailer park."

Tears blurred Mary's eyes as the truth of her friend's words struck home. She was just a child, and she already knew how fair the law was with those who were victims. Her only chance was to run. "Can I write to you Myra?"

"I wouldn't do that" Myra said. "That just gives the police a lead on where you are, plus I'll have to show your letters to someone else."

"Why Myra?" Mary asked.

" 'Cause I can't read" she said without shame. "Our school ain't open enough to do me much good."

"Myra, some day I'm coming back for you" Mary said with resolve. "If you need me when I come back I'll take care of you. That's a promise."

"Oh poo, you just git out of here before the law comes knockin' or I'll be the one takin' care of you" Myra said and wiped her eyes with the back of her hand. "And take this with you" she added, pulling a coin from her pocket and thrusting it into Mary's palm. "This is all I got."

Mary looked in her hand. Myra had given her a nickel.

NINE

The sealed life in the trailer park suddenly didn't look so bad as Mary walked slowly along State Route 19 headed North. Where the route took her she had no idea, but at least it was in the general direction that Myra recommended and hopefully led away from prison. She was worried about things like finding food and shelter, but somehow there was no guilt concerning the killing of Ray Don. She wished it had not been her, but knew he was an evil man and would have hurt more people had he lived.

A flat bed truck rumbled by, the first vehicle she had seen in hours, and it paused at a four way stop sign before moving through. The ancient vehicle rattled like an old man with emphysema and coughed a loud plume of black smoke out of a rusted tail pipe as it attempted to gain speed. With a loud bang under the dented bird wings hood, the engine died.

The driver's side door flew open with a groan and a small man in work clothes and wearing a sweat stained straw hat leaped to the ground swearing in Spanish. He threw open one side of the hood and stuck his head near the engine, turning and twisting a thick wire. Mary ran to the back of the truck, which was loaded with a huge mound of straw, and quickly burrowed inside. She lay still until she heard the engine bark into life and felt a lurch as the truck moved ahead.

Despite a gnawing hunger, fatigue took her to unconsciousness and nightmares. She was running from Ray Don, his breath hot and angry on her neck, but her feet sank into mud that refused her forward progress. Pumping

her arms and slipping in the sticky ooze, Mary screamed as
his hand clamped down on her shoulder. She struggled to
break free, but the iron grip shook her like a fish in a bear's
mouth.

"Senorita, wake up please" a voice insisted.

Mary opened her eyes and saw the driver of the
truck standing on the ground as he shook her shoulder. The
man had pulled the straw away from her face and was close
enough that she could smell garlic on his breath. Her
stomach rumbled a reminder of its hunger. "I'm sorry" she
said, sitting upright and causing a small shower of straw.

"No, no, it is fine" the man said in heavily accented
Spanish. "I heard you yelling and crying from inside the
truck and I say, either my straw is haunted or someone has
hitched a ride." He smiled at his own humor, crinkling his
eyes and displaying perfect white teeth. "I found you yelling
in your sleep, so I say to myself, I say Manuel, thees girl
she is having a bad dream. Then I say to myself, why is
there a girl in my straw?" He spread his arms and shrugged
his shoulders in question, the good humor showing on his
handsome face.

"Do you have any food?" Mary asked, desperation
crowding out shame or shyness.

"Oh, indeed I do Senorita" Manuel said. "I have a
salami and a loaf of my Juanita's home baked bread. She
makes bread that even someone who is full would eat just
to taste such a delight. Come, you ride with me in the front
seat and share my salami and bread."

Mary scrambled from the pile of straw, brushing
golden dust and dry pieces from her clothes. She shook
her head and a shower of straw fell from her hair. The smell
of the salami wafted out of the open windows of the truck,
instantly making her stomach rumble in protest and saliva
filled her mouth. She jumped into the truck and pulled the
door closed, eyes locked on a two foot long piece of salami
and a loaf of bread toasted to a golden brown. Only pure
determination prevented her from grabbing both and biting

off chunks.

Manuel joined her and pulled a knife from a sheath on his belt. He sliced a three inch long piece of meat and then tore a large chunk of bread from the loaf. He wiped the blade on his trousers, replaced the knife, then offered the bread and salami to Mary. "Start with this you hungry little gringo" he said, "but go slow. If you gulp it down it will come right back up and then it is wasted. You may have more after this, so just take your time."

Mary obeyed as best she could, forcing her hands into her lap after each bite, but she thought perhaps nothing had ever tasted this good. Her host was as good as his word, because immediately following her last bite he cut new and even bigger pieces than before.

"How long has it been since you've eaten Nino" he asked, a frown of concern resting on his face.

Swallowing first to be polite after a bite, Mary said "It seems like days, but I guess I got used to not having much to eat. When I get an opportunity, I guess I overdo it a bit. It's been like that pretty much all of my life."

"Where is your family while all of this hunger is going on" Manuel asked. He started the old truck's engine and lurched forward again as he spoke.

"They're dead" she said without hesitation, noting that Manuel did not seem surprised or shocked. As for herself, Mary didn't wonder in the least where they were going or why this man was so kind. Her stomach was no longer empty, she was well rested, and the horrors of her past life were moving mile after mile away. For the first time in a very long time she felt safe, despite the uncertainty of her future. She enjoyed the landscape as the old truck rattled along, admiring mostly fields of tobacco, soy beans and corn. She waved at a doe and her fawn who stood at the edge of a stand of trees, eyeing the rattling truck with suspicion. Mary's wave sent them darting quickly into the woods and the comforting cover of pine boughs.

Eventually she drifted off to sleep again, feeling a

comfort and warmth which drained her of stress and fear. The backfire of the old truck as it tried to shut down gracefully woke her from a dreamless slumber. Steam rose from the front of the vehicle like a dragon hissing at a knight on his faithful steed. She blinked the last remnants of sleep from her eyes and looked about. They were in a small town, the main street looking like the picture on a nickel post card. The store fronts were old and yet neat and tidy, the First National Bank standing out because it was built with white granite stone instead of wood like the buildings which surrounded it on all sides.

Flannery's General Store and The Mayfair Hotel caught her eye as well as Ruby's Diner, the shabbiest yet busiest place on the block. A seemingly steady stream of people traded places in and out of the audibly creaking front door, all exchanging nods and pleasant comments as they passed. Mary stretched like a cat, arching her back, pointing her toes, and reaching her fingers toward the floorboards of the truck. She rolled her neck in a circular motion, loosening the kinks from the awkward position in which she had been sleeping.

A yawn opened her mouth wide, breath escaping in a luxurious, garlic perfumed whoosh, when her eyes fell on the building outside the truck window. She froze in place, the yawn catching almost painfully in her throat as she read: Brecksville, Ohio Police Station. Service, Loyalty, Protection. Manuel had climbed out of the truck and was waving to a man in a light brown uniform. He was tall and lean, middle aged but athletic looking, like a former high school quarterback. A round badge with a number in the middle and the word Sheriff winding around the edge in a half moon was pinned on his starched shirt. A standard issue black leather police utility belt was strapped as tight as a corset around his middle. A mahogany pistol grip stuck out of the black leather holster.

The two men were talking in hushed tones, glancing over from time to time in an obvious gesture that they were talking about her. Mary felt betrayed, angry with herself for trusting this kindly man who was calmly turning her over to the authorities. She considered running, but quickly rejected that as she studied the sheriff's athletic build. Besides, even if she did outrun the man, he would have a network of police following her in no time. Escape was futile and prison likely, but she felt no regrets or guilt for protecting herself from Ray Don.

The sheriff moved to her open window, placed a palm at each corner of the opening, then bent over to look at Mary face to face. His look was friendly and even warm, a smile playing near the corners of his lips. He smelled of Ivory soap, Old Spice and starch. "Hello young lady" he said softly. His voice was easy and nonthreatening yet firm and controlled. "My name is Ed Jenkins. I'm the sheriff here in Brecksville, at least for one more year until the new elections." He smiled now, showing even white teeth and twinkling eyes of mirth and orneriness. "And what might your name be?"

"Mary....." she hesitated, almost blurting out her last name. Then her mind went as blank as a slate chalkboard on the first day of school and she could not for the life of her think of a fictitious last name.

"Well, Mary" Sheriff Jenkins said without flinching, "my friend Manuel tells me you're looking for a place to stay and maybe a job. Is that a fair statement for him to make?"

"Yes sir, I guess that's the gosh awful truth he told you" Mary answered, hope pulling excitement to the surface and showing in her voice.

"Well, why don't you climb on out of the truck and come inside" the sheriff said. "We'll get you settled in and then see about work. I've got an idea that I know just the thing you're looking for."

Mary followed him inside the small office and jail, nervous but not wanting to appear uneasy. Sheriff Jenkins led her to a small cell with a bed, a toilet with no lid or seat, and a small sink with a single cold water faucet. He gestured to the inside of the cell and Mary paused, looking up at him with apprehension.

"I know it's not much" he said, "but at least it's a bed and a roof over your head until you try out a job. We'll leave the cell door open so you won't feel like you're locked up, and I'll have a couple prisoners hang some blankets so you've got a little privacy."

Hesitating, Mary touched the cold iron bars, their immovable strength daring entrance and then escape. She swallowed hard and tried to step in but her feet refused to move.

As if an imaginary light bulb clicked on Sheriff Jenkins suddenly understood. He moved back one step to give Mary more room and then he smiled. "This is not a trick Mary. If I wanted to lock you in a cell I could easily accomplish that. I'm offering you a place to sleep for a few nights until we see if the job I have in mind for you works out. No tricks, no lies. No one is going to hurt you." He knitted his brow and the smile faded. "I have a feeling you've been lied to and hurt quite a bit in the past. Well, that doesn't happen in my town. If you're ever in trouble I'll come and talk to you about it, then we'll decide together what to do. Is that fair enough?"

Mary's answer was to walk into the cell and sit on the bunk. She looked up into the sheriff's eyes, not with trust, because it would be a ling time before she ever trusted again, but with resignation. He would do what he would do. She gave him a warm smile and said, "Thank you Sheriff Jenkins. I appreciate your kindness."

He smiled in return. "You get some rest, because I'll be getting you up at five o'clock in the morning. I'll take you to your new job and you can start earning your keep."

Mary didn't ask what the job was, it really didn't matter. She just curled up on the bunk and stared at the open door until she fell asleep.

TEN

A gentle shake woke Mary from a dreamless sleep at exactly five o'clock the following morning. Sheriff Jenkins stepped away as her eyes flew open in a moment of terror. The cell door was open as he promised and someone had hung the wool blankets across the bars while Mary slept. Another thick, scratchy, gray wool blanket with U.S. Army stenciled on one side had been placed over her for warmth and security. She could smell moth balls and actually enjoyed the warm, scratchy and fragrant covering.

The sheriff led her to a small room with four shower stalls. He placed a stern looking deputy at the door to guarantee her privacy and pointed to a brown sack with Flannery's General Store printed on the outside. "Everything in that sack is for you" he said and left the room. He pulled the door closed and she heard him walk down the hall, the metal heel plates on his boots clacking on the cement.

Mary found a bar of soap, a small bottle of shampoo, a comb, a toothbrush and toothpaste in the bag. She gasped in surprise and her heart leaped in excitement when she found socks, underwear, a new pair of Levi's that were just a bit large but manageable, and a Pendleton shirt with black and red checks. The most incredible thing, however, was at the bottom of the bag like a special treat hidden until last. There was a pair of black Converse canvas shoes that fit like they were especially made for Mary Johnson.

She forced herself to linger in the shower, making sure she was squeaky clean before putting on the new

clothes. Her brown hair looked almost blonde with dust
and dirt washed away, and she pulled the comb through her
tangles despite the pain in her hurry to get dressed.

Soon she was admiring herself in a cracked full
length mirror hanging on one wall. Only the jeans were a
bit too long, but she just turned up the bottom of each leg
two rolls and they rested just below the edge of the top of
each shoe. When she opened the door she tried not to strut
down the hall but supposed she failed in the attempt.

Sheriff Jenkins was sitting at his desk studying a
wanted poster when she paused at his open door. He glanced
up and then smiled at the sight of her. "Well now, look
what we have here" he said. "You look like a new person."

"Thank you so much Sheriff Jenkins" Mary
bubbled, feeling the world was turning her way. "I'll pay
you back for the clothes, I swear I will."

"We won't worry about paybacks" he said. "Just
look at this as a welcome to our little town. You know, a
place this size needs new blood, especially young people."
He touched her arm with his index finger which drew her
eyes to his face. "Mary, I want you to know that if you ever
want to tell me anything about your past, I'll do all I can to
help you."

Mary felt the color drain from her face and her
heart increased its beat. "I don't have anything about my
past to talk about. I mean, there's nothing" she blurted out
anxiously.

"That's fine, that's fine" he soothed. "I just want
you to know I'm your friend and I can help you if you're
ever in need."

"Okay Sheriff, thanks" Mary replied, relaxing a bit.

"Are you ready to go to work this morning?" he
asked, changing the subject and ushering her toward the
door at the same time.

"I sure am, but where are we going?" she said. "I've
been wondering since you told me, and I am really anxious
to get myself established."

They walked outside into the fresh morning breeze, a huge red ball of sun just beginning to climb over the rooftop of the closest building. The sheriff gestured toward Ruby's Diner and nodded his head. "There it is Mary, Ruby's Diner. Ruby hasn't had help or any time off for about twenty five years, and I think I've finally got her convinced to let the right person help her. I hope you're that person, because I believe you two need each other."

They walked into the small eatery, Sheriff Jenkins ignoring the closed sign and ushering Mary inside. A dozen wonderful aromas assaulted her nose as they walked toward the small kitchen area behind the front counter. A tiny woman stood with her back to them, working furiously with several huge, steaming pots, mounds of potatoes, and bacon on an open grill. She was thin as paper, shoulders hunched forward in an emaciated stance of a famine survivor.

Mary and Sheriff Jenkins stopped at the counter, he perching one hip on a stool and she standing quietly by the open space that led to the work area. Mary leaned slightly forward as if in anticipation of helping but stayed behind the imaginary line that separated customers from employees. The little woman obviously knew they were there because she turned ever so slightly toward them, viewing her guests like a predator trying to pretend she didn't know her prey was near. Mary saw an unfiltered cigarette hanging from the woman's lips like a piece of chalk, an inch long piece of ash bending down in a silent homage to gravity.

Lines etched her face like a Van Gogh painting, seeming to be expertly cut into place to add character to her age. When she turned away Mary saw the ash fall into a boiling pot, but the old woman didn't even flinch. She continued cooking the mounds of food as if nothing else on earth mattered.

The sheriff gestured to a stool at the counter and Mary sat nervously on the circular seat, suppressing the temptation to push off with her hand and spin in circles.

Sheriff Jenkins slid off his stool, walked behind the counter, and took two coffee cups from a pyramid of mud colored china stacked to the right of the griddle. He poured coffee, black and steamy, and set one cup in front of Mary. He lifted two plates from a stack beside the cups and picked up a wide spatula from a pile of wide spoons, tongs, oversize forks, and strainers. He spooned two healthy portions of potatoes on each plate and then turned two runny eggs, each upside down, on top of that. He sat one in front of Mary and the other by his coffee cup. Forks appeared like a magician pulling them from under the counter and without a word they each ate every bite, seeming to race each other to finish first.

When they finished, Mary gathered the dishes and boldly walked behind the counter. An empty tub sat beside an identical container filled with soapy water. Next to it was a tub of clear, hot, rinse water. Mary washed and dried everything and replaced each item in its original spot. She then went back to her perch at the counter.

The woman turned from her cooking, scowling at them as if angry. She squinted one eye almost closed, the smoke from her cigarette lifting lazily to curl around the hooded lid. She looked much older than she actually was, hard living and a generally sour disposition combining to hasten wrinkles. No makeup, gray hair, and leathery skin accented her unattractiveness. Mary remembered her mother saying 'There's no excuse for a woman not combing her hair and putting a little paint on the barn.' This woman not only did nothing to help her appearance, she seemed to work hard to make herself look worse.

She stepped over to the sheriff and placed two beet red, work worn hands flat on the counter top. Ashes drifted from the end of the cigarette and floated like dirty snowflakes in a pattern around her splayed fingers. "Those meals will cost you four bits. Each" she added.

Sheriff Jenkins pulled a money clip with several folded bills from his pocket and peeled a dollar bill like skin on an onion from the grip of the clip. He tossed it on the counter and the old woman snatched it from the green Linoleum surface and stuffed it in her apron pocket. The sheriff nodded toward Mary and said, "Ruby, this is Mary, the girl I told you about. She's ready to go to work this morning if you're still willing to have her."

Ruby glared at Mary through the haze of smoke swirling around her eyes and nodded toward the far corner of the diner. "Start back there in that corner and move forward. Clean everything that don't move for at least one minute and when you're done I want to be able to serve food on it. Cleaning supplies are in the shed out back." Without another word she turned away and tended the large cooking area. Mary slid off her stool and accepted a grin and a wink from Sheriff Jenkins. She walked back and hurried out to the small, sun bleached shed at the rear of the diner. Most of the cleaning equipment looked new, which was not surprising when she saw how dirty the little restaurant had become. Layers of grease covered everything, quite simply from years of cooking and patrons who smoked. Even the walls were slick to the touch, so Mary stood on a chair in the corner, began with the ceiling, and worked her way down.

She changed water in the bucket she used to rinse her scrub brush and rags every ten minutes. Each time the water looked like a puddle on a dirt road. Everything changed color as she worked, the cherry blue and white decor coming alive as it was cleaned. Sunlight streamed through the large front window which had become translucent over the years as dirt piled on top of itself.

Barely one tenth of the job was complete when the customers came flowing in, all friendly and curious as they saw this newcomer working like a person possessed. She met Stan Kenton, the president of The First National Bank. He told her he was from The First National Bank because it was the only national bank. Charlie Newton, the manager of the Mayfair Hotel, told her he was a regular for breakfast. When Fred Flannery, the owner of the general store came in to meet her she paused long enough to show him the new clothes from his store.

"By golly, if I'd known how good those old things would look on a pretty girl, I'd have charged twice the price on 'em" he said with a broad grin.

"I really appreciate your generosity Mr. Flannery" Mary said. "This is a very kind thing you did for me."

He blushed and waved away her compliment. "Shoot, it wasn't much. Besides, folks need to help one another when they can."

"Well, I certainly appreciate it anyway" she said. "I would like to pay you for the clothes when I can."

Flannery moved toward an empty table with another wave and said, "Little lady, if I let you pay me money then I'd lose the good feelin' I have about helpin' you, so I guess I'm too selfish to let you take that away. You just come shopin' when you need to buy somethin' and I'll appreciate your business."

"You'll sure have it" Mary promised.

It seemed that the entire town ate at Ruby's, flowing in and out in a steady stream all morning. The routine was the same for each customer. They went to the counter and placed an order which Ruby acknowledged with a curt nod and a shower of ashes. She prepared the order and sat it on the counter while the customer got coffee or juice themselves and waited patiently at a table. Ruby would bellow the first name of the appropriate customer when the food was ready and each person picked it up themselves. After eating, the customers stacked dirty dishes in two deep tubs behind the counter and then stepped to the huge cash register sitting on the far end of the counter. Some waited patiently until Ruby came over, took their money, and opened the cash register with a loud ca-ching. Others would open the register themselves, put in a bill, take out change, then leave without a word. Seldom did anyone ask what they owed and Mary didn't see a menu or posted prices anywhere.

    Ruby flipped the OPEN sign over to CLOSED at nine thirty, although people came in from time to time and self served coffee. Ruby ignored them and started making hamburger patties and cooked huge pots of beef and noodles for lunch. She waved at Mary who was about one quarter through with her cleaning. "Dishes" Ruby grunted as if the word caused pain when it blew past her lips.

    Mary washed, rinsed, and dried dishes for an hour, then changed the water in the two sinks in preparation for more dishes. The OPEN sign was again displayed at eleven o'clock and by eleven thirty the same crowd was coming in for lunch. She continued her cleaning, covering three foot square sections from ceiling to floor. The customers automatically avoided the area she had cleaned, crowding into the familiar greasy tables and chairs, even waiting for a table instead of being the first to defile Mary's antiseptic surfaces.

    Ruby finally glanced around, did a double take, then spread her feet and placed curled fists against each hip, looking every bit like an enraged drill sergeant. "What in the stinkin' heck are you people doin' millin' around the front door like that. There's tables as empty as the Gobi Desert over there and you all are actin' like none of them have ever been cleaned before. Now git over there and sit down before you all put an old woman out of business." She maintained her pose as the chastised customers moved gingerly across the cleaned line. They looked uncomfortable as they tried to keep their feet still and didn't touch the tops of the tables. "For crin' out loud I should dump table scraps all over the floor" Ruby mumbled and went back to her cooking.

    Fortunately the uneasiness was soon forgotten and the restaurant soon buzzed with conversation and resumed the sound of metal utensils bumping china plates. Mary smiled to her self, bemused and yet impressed by the concern the townspeople showed in her work.

William B. Keller

The CLOSED sign appeared again at two o'clock and Mary did the dishes again, this time without being asked. Ruby cleaned the huge cooking surface herself, turning the gas burners on high and pushing a towel soaked in lemon juice and water over the hot surface. She used a pancake flipper to propel the steaming cloth, finally turning the gas jets off with a flourish. The diner was clean three fourths of the way across, a visible line showing where Mary's efforts had been interrupted.

Ruby dropped wearily into a chair at one of the freshly cleaned tables and motioned for Mary to sit in one herself. She lit a cigarette from the glowing end of her last smoke before crushing it out in a gleaming, transparent glass ashtray. "Do you work this hard every day Honey or are you just trying to impress me today" Ruby asked after taking a deep drag of smoke. Little puffs escaped as she talked.

"I wanted to impress you" Mary said truthfully. "The fact is I do work hard, but if every day was as hard as this one, I don't know how long I would last."

Ruby laughed, a deep rattle bubbling from her lungs at the same time. "Hard working and honest. By crackers that's rare to find anywhere. If you keep it that way, I'd say you might have a job here for a while. That's if, of course, you want it."

"Oh yes Ma'am I do" Mary quickly answered. "I need a job if I'm to make my own way."

"Well, you have a one day start. There's a door off the bathroom in back. Clean the toilet and sink and then use this key." Ruby pulled a key from her apron and tossed it on the table. "That key unlocks the door and you'll find a room with a bed, a lamp, a table and chair, and an old radio that might still work. That's your room to stay in until I tell you otherwise. I'll stop by and tell Ed Jenkins you've moved." She pushed to her feet with a wince of pain on her face. "I won't have no girl of mine living in jail like a common criminal."

Moving slowly to the door, Ruby looked back at Mary as she pulled the door closed. "By the way, I've not had a day off in thirty years. You'll find recipes for tomorrow's meals over by the cash register. Start cooking at five, be ready by six thirty for the first rush. Take the money at the end of the day to Ed. He'll bring it to me at the house. If you have any problems, well you'll just have to work them out." She closed the door and was gone.

Mary was too stunned to react. She was frightened, then angry, then frightened again. She ran to the door to call out after Ruby, then shook her head and simply went to work. First she finished cleaning the diner, working without pause until everything sparkled like new. Next she studied the recipes detailed in a neat and legible cursive style on three by five inch note cards. Mary inventoried the supplies, premeasured everything that could be prepared overnight, and finally peeled and sliced bags of potatoes which she put in cooking pots and covered with water. Everything possible was in place by midnight.

Finally she cleaned the bathroom and unlocked the door just across the narrow hall. A small but lovely room with the furnishings Ruby had promised were within. A key wind Big Ben alarm clock sat on its wide spread metal legs on the dresser at the end of the bed. Mary sat the alarm for four thirty and dropped into bed. She was asleep in moments.

ELEVEN

Someone once said every person has that perfect thing they are able to do. Not everyone finds their niche in life, which is unfortunate, but for those that do their success is assured. Mary Johnson discovered she could run a restaurant.

Sheriff Jenkins turned the sign over to OPEN when he came in for his breakfast. Mary moved with precision from piles of potatoes to mounds of sausage and bacon, barely pausing to smile and wave at the sheriff as she prepared his plate of fried potatoes, sausage links, and scrambled eggs. He nodded in admiration as he filled a coffee cup and looked around the sparkling clean diner. Not even a speck of dust lay on a table, the salt and pepper shakers freshly filled after a washing for the first time in years. The metal napkin holders were polished and almost hurt the eyes as light bounced like a reflection in a mirror from the surfaces.

Not a word was spoken until Sheriff Jenkins finished his breakfast and deposited his plate and fork in the pan behind the counter. He rang open the cash register and deposited his money, then closed the drawer with a flourish. "I trust I am your first paying customer" he said with a smile.

"And so you are Sheriff Jenkins" Mary said as she broke four eggs at once and deftly dropped each onto the hot griddle.

"I would consider it a favor if you just called me Ed" he said. "That's what my friends call me and most everyone in town is my friend."

"I would consider it an honor to have you as a friend Sher..., I mean Ed" Mary said. She looked over her shoulder as the door opened and five men walked in. "Good morning gentlemen" she called out. "Step right up and place your order, and if you will please tell me your names. It might take me a spell to remember everyone."

A tall, thin man with a nose hooked like the beak of an eagle frowned as he took his place in front of the counter. "Where's Ruby?" he demanded, looking around the small diner as if he expected her to pop out like a magic trick.

"She took a little time off, so I'm filling in for her" Mary answered with a smile. "I'm Mary" she added.

A portly, red faced man with a grin that made his eyes disappear touched an imaginary hat brim with two fingers. "I'm Seth Burgess Ma'am. I'm pleased to meet you and I'll have four eggs over easy with a pile of those potatoes to go with them."

"I just dropped four on the griddle Seth, so it will just be a minute" Mary said with her brightest smile.

"I don't understand why Ruby's not here" the thin man grumbled. "Ruby's always here."

Another man pushed forward and gave Mary a smile and a nod. "Pete Sandburg here Mary. I'll take bacon, potatoes, and a scoop of them scrambled eggs if you please." He turned to the first man and shook his head. "Heck fire Elrod, I'd think you'd be happy that you're gonna get breakfast not only from a pretty girl but there won't be no ashes in it."

Mary smiled even broader and shook a curl from her eyes. "Why, thank you Pete. For those kind words you'll find an extra strip of bacon under those potatoes." She filled two plates and sat them, steamy hot, on the counter.

"Well look at that" Seth Burgess said, "we didn't even have to sit and wait for ten minutes. Little Lady, you tell Ruby she's fired."

Mary laughed, a pleasant sound with no pretense. "I'm afraid I'm the hired help around here Seth. No one is going to replace Ruby. She's just taking a well earned day off."

"Well, I guess she deserves it" the thin man said, a bit put out at the attention his friends were getting. "She's not had a day off for as long as I can remember."

"Right you are Elrod" Mary said, turning her charm on her toughest customer. "Now what can I prepare for you today? Oh, and by the way, if you get the same thing every morning I'll have your plate ready when you walk through the door."

Elrod blushed with pride that she knew his name after a casual mention from his friend, and puffed out his chest at the thought of being served 'the usual' because he was a regular customer. "Well, in that case I'd like two sunny side eggs, one sausage link, one strip of bacon, and potatoes" he said. "And that would be fine every morning" he finished in a tone of authority. "I'll be in Monday through Saturday right about this time."

"Done and done" Mary agreed, dropping more eggs on the griddle as she spoke. "I hope we might see you for lunch from time to time too" she added.

"You can count on that" Elrod said with a smile.

By the end of the morning Mary had met nearly everyone in town, many of them coming in to satisfy their curiosity and meet this young stranger who had taken over Ruby's diner. The day flew by and she found the work completed and the next day's menu prepared by four thirty in the afternoon.

A canvas bag behind the cash register with the First National Bank imprinted on its front seemed the obvious carrier for the day's receipts. Mary emptied the curved slots and pulled a rawhide string on top of the bag to secure the contents. She walked over to the sheriff's office whistling a familiar tune. Ed Jenkins sat behind his desk, feet propped on its scarred top, reading a stack of bulletin's from the State Highway Patrol. He waved as Mary came in the door, not moving his boots from their perch.

"Good evening Ed" she said. "Ruby wanted me to bring the money from today over to you. She said you would take it to her."

"Uh huh" he replied, still concentrating on the bulletins. "Ruby called me earlier and asked me to bring you and the money to her house. Give me a minute while I finish up this stack of wanted bulletins and we'll go." He leafed through the notices with a practiced eye, then paused with a frown as one obviously caught his attention. Slowly he pulled his feet from the desk top and leaned forward until his elbows rested where his feet had been. He lay the stack aside with the exception of one. He glanced up repeatedly as he read, a troubled look on his face.

Mary began to feel uneasy as the silence lengthened, realizing something was wrong but not able to identify quite what was happening. She dropped her eyes and studied the worn floor as she waited.

"You know" he finally said, "I wonder what would make a child attack her parent."

She looked up without hesitation and held his eyes without wavering. "I would suppose a girl might protect herself if a man tried to, well, tried to force himself on her. Especially if it wasn't the first time."

His gaze also did not waver. "I believe if I saw a man doing that to his daughter I might be inclined to use a knife on him myself" he said softly.

"Maybe" she said, "but I don't guess that makes it any more right."

"Oh, I think maybe it does" he answered, crumpling the flier into a ball and dropping it into a waste basket.

"Did it say this girl is wanted for murder?" she asked, her hands sweating and trembling slightly.

"It just says she's wanted for questioning in an attack" he said. "Either the man didn't die or he was still alive when the bulletin went out. Sometimes all the details aren't available so they report what they've got."

"I see" she said, then swallowed in an attempt to slow her hammering heart. "Do you have any questions?"

Sheriff Jenkins tossed the remaining wanted notices on a corner of his desk. He smiled and shook his head, pushing to his feet and moving toward the door. "No, I sure don't have any questions, just a comment. You're the best thing to happen for Ruby in years. She's not real healthy and Doc Simmons has been after her for some time to slow down, but in a town this size it's not easy to find the right person. It's a tough job and most folks don't want to make the commitment."

"And you think I will?" Mary asked.

He led her out the door and held the door open on the passenger side of the squad car. He waited until he climbed in behind the wheel to answer. "I think you need a new start in life and that makes you much more likely to take on a big challenge. You've already made that place fit to be in and the whole town's buzzing about the way you charmed the socks off everyone who came in the place." He pulled the car from the curb and drove toward the far end of town. "I think you're going to do just fine here Mary Johnson."

Mary turned to him and touched his arm. "I haven't told anyone my name. Would it be possible to keep it that way?"

He nodded but didn't answer until he pulled in front of a large two story brick home and turned off the engine. "I understand. In fact, this could be a bit of fun for the folks here in town. Sooner or later everyone will be trying to figure out why you don't use your last name. You might find it easier to make one up."

"No, I don't want to lie" Mary said. "My life has had too many of them and I don't want to add more."

"Fair enough" Sheriff Jenkins said and opened his car door, "handle it any way you want. I'll not tell anyone.

There's Ruby's place, she's expecting us."

They walked in silence up the brick walkway to the heavy oak front door. A tarnished brass knocker, a lion's head with a thick brass ring in its mouth, made a hollow booming sound inside the house like the sound effects in a low budget horror movie. The door even ominously creaked as it opened into the front parlor of Ruby's home.

The smell of must and stale cigarette smoke sprang out like a lurking predator as they stepped into the dimly lit entry. Ruby was wearing a tattered robe tied loosely around a floor length flannel nightshirt. The ever-present cigarette hung like a bent white finger from the center of her lips. She coughed, a wet gurgling sound, and waved at them to follow. Sheriff Jenkins closed the door and they walked behind Ruby in silence.

She led them to a surprisingly pleasant room with a fireplace and shelves filled with books. A large oriental rug was centered on highly polished tongue in groove oak flooring, and a leather sofa with two matching chairs faced the hearth of the fireplace. Several scented candles flickered as they brought in a gentle brush of air, their vanilla scent almost covering the tobacco. Ruby moved to a chair and fell heavily onto the leather cushion, the movement causing air to rush out like a whoopee cushion. Mary and Sheriff Jenkins took a position on the sofa.

"Well, I gather you survived the diner" Ruby said, the hint of a smile tugging at her mouth.

"Yes Ma'am, it went quite well" Mary answered. "We brought the money from the cash register as you asked."

Ruby counted the money before speaking again. "Well, it would appear that you had an exceptional day. There's over double a normal day's receipts in here."

"I think people were curious about me" Mary answered. "I met pretty close to the total number of people who live in this town, and a lot of them obviously didn't know the usual routine of how to place orders and pick up food."

"And how did you handle that" Ruby asked through a blue haze of smoke.

"I called them up to the counter and explained it to them. It's not hard, and everyone was nice about it."

"The new people wouldn't have known prices" Ruby said. "What did you do about that?"

Mary relaxed now, ready and able to answer any question concerning the way she handled the diner. "I watched the regulars, discretely of course, put money in the register. After three or four put in the same amount for different combinations of orders, I knew the prices. When someone asked I could tell them. I also handled the cash register for the new customers."

Ruby smiled now, leaning back into the chair cushions and appearing to burrow in like a mole. "You memorized all the combinations and prices in a day?"

"Well, actually it took about an hour for the breakfast crowd and closer to two hours for the lunch session, but we were busier at noon and I had less time to concentrate on prices."

Ruby laughed outright now, bending forward and slapping her hands on her bony knees. The laughter caused a fit of coughing which Mary feared would cause her to strangle, but she regained control at about the time her face began to turn purple. Gasping for air she roared, "Girl, you've got to be the best restaurateur since, since, well since me." She howled with laughter again until her air passages filled with phlegm, and finally Ruby sank back exhausted in her chair. "Oh my, I just love this. You are a prize, I tell you an absolute prize."

Mary didn't know if she should smile, laugh, frown, be angry, or what she should do, so she just said quietly, "Thank you."

"Here's the deal honey" Ruby said, all business again and lighting a cigarette with the butt of the last one. "You're running my diner from now on until I say otherwise.

I may or may not come in, that will be up to me. There's a book behind the register with a list of my food suppliers. Order what you need and learn quick. I don't like waste. Ed will bring you deposit slips for the bank, so you can start doing a daily bank run. I'll call Stan Kenton tomorrow and we'll let the bank pay all the bills. If you need anything you see him, Fred Flannery at the general store, or Ed here." She nodded at the sheriff. "If you think the world is going to end, and honey it better be, then you come here and see me, otherwise I don't want to see or hear anything about that diner except for the bank statement. You got any questions?"

Only about a million was what went through Mary's mind, but she said "No Ma'am."

"Then everyone get out of here and give me peace" she barked.

Sheriff Jenkins waited until they reached his car before he started laughing. "Well, I would say so long as you run a tight ship and don't bother her, you're the new manager of Ruby's Diner."

"Do you think she realizes how young I am and that I don't have much schooling?" Mary asked, her head swirling.

"Mary, you're more grown up than three fourths of the adults in this town, and you're brighter than ninety percent of them. I would suggest you not worry about a thing."

Despite herself, Mary smiled. This could be the turning point in her life, the chance she had been looking for. After being kicked in the face by fate all her life, maybe this was when things changed. Surely everyone's luck changes sooner or later.

"What are you thinking about" Sheriff Jenkins asked.

"I'm thinking maybe my luck has changed" she said.

He pulled the car to the curb in front of the diner and nodded toward the front door. "What you did when you went in there was not luck Mary. It was hard work and brains."

She opened the door and smiled at him. "Thanks" she said and stepped from the car.

Sheriff Jenkins held up his hand as she prepared to push the car door shut. She leaned down to look at him when he spoke. "You earned this opportunity Mary. Never apologize for what you earn."

Mary nodded and closed the car door. She watched his tail lights until they disappeared around a corner. She sighed and turned toward the diner. Squaring her shoulders, she went inside.

Part Two

TWELVE

Mary didn't need to look over her shoulder to know who walked through the door of the diner at ten minutes before six. She heard the soft clunk as the OPEN side of the sign was flopped over in the window. This routine had been exactly the same each Monday through Saturday for the last ten years. The eggs were cooked to perfection and the potatoes filled every other open spot on the plate as she scooped the man sized meal and turned to place it on the counter just as Sheriff Jenkins took a seat.

"We're going to have a hot one I think" he said as he grabbed a fork. He had changed very little in ten years, just a hint of gray around the temples and a new line or two on his face reminded Mary that time had marched forward.

"I like it hot" she said. "Maybe it's the hours I spend cooking. When you're hot all the time maybe you get used to it."

"Mmm, may be" he said around a mouthful of eggs. He couldn't help but notice how Mary had changed. She was a woman now, slender but filled out like a fashion model with curves. For the thousandth time he wished he were fifteen years younger, although he wasn't sure that would make a difference. Every young buck in town, and quite a few from other towns had tried to capture Mary's attention, but all had failed in their quest. She worked, visited elderly people and was active in the nearby Mormon Church. Sheriff Jenkins never knew her to go on a date or even share a ride, Dutch treat, to the movies with a man. Her church work seemed to fulfill her, and even the single men there could make no headway.

"Pat Conroy was in yesterday morning" she said. "He told me he was going to run against you in the next election."

Sheriff Jenkins laughed, then choked on a mouthful of potatoes. He lifted a hand when Mary started around the counter to pound his back. "I'm okay" he gasped, face as red as a tomato. "That's just the funniest thing I think I've heard in weeks. Do you know why Pat is suddenly running for office?"

"Not the slightest idea" Mary said with a smile. "There's been no one foolish enough to run against you for two terms, so I wondered why Pat Conroy of all people thought he might have a chance."

"He's mad because I found his still" the sheriff chuckled. "He put it way out on the old Slane place so far up a big hill covered with scrub oak that it practically takes a mountain goat to get up there."

"How did you find it" Mary asked as she started a third fifty cup coffee maker.

"There's only one place in the County where scrub oaks grow, because farmers keep them out of the fields. The Slane place is vacant, so there's no nosy people checking up on anyone, and that ground is so poor anyway that when Elmer was alive he let anything grow up there. I knew when I saw Pat's truck with a scrub oak wedged up under the wheel well I could find his still."

"Why, I do believe you are a regular Sherlock Holmes" Mary said with real admiration. "But how did you know Pat was making moonshine?"

"Oh, that was probably the worst kept secret in the County" he said. "The liquor store did everything but stock his Mason jars on their shelf. Pat was so sure I couldn't find the still he wasn't even too quiet about the thing when I was around."

"So are you going to arrest him?" Mary asked.

"Heavens no" he said as he finished his last bite. "I hurt him more by smashing a lot of expensive equipment than a jail term would ever do. Besides, Pat has a wife and three kids. If he isn't going to work at the mill they're going to be out on the street. I don't want to be a part of that."

Mary smiled fondly. This big man had to be the finest person she had ever known. She long ago promised herself that a man would never harm her again, and the only way she could prevent it was to avoid a relationship. Still, if any man could be an exception, this was the one. She almost told him, right at that moment, but instead said "I think we're a lucky town to have you as our sheriff. You've always looked at what was right instead of what was the law."

He blushed, thinking about the time years ago when he threw away Mary's wanted bulletin. "Oh, I don't know Mary. Pat would probably rather I throw him in jail. That way he wouldn't have to push logs all day and worry about crying babies all night."

Mary chuckled and added a dozen eggs on the grill. The morning rush was about three minutes away. "Other than Pat, do you expect any opposition?"

"No one has registered, including Pat" he said. "I almost wish someone else would challenge me so I could at least know if it's that no one else can beat me or if no one else wants the job."

The diner's door opened and closed twice in a matter of moments and Mary grabbed two plates. She looked over her shoulder and called out, "Morning Charlie. And how are you today Judge Wamble?" Then to the sheriff, "I think we all know the answer to your question Ed, even if you want to pretend you don't."

Almost immediately the diner was too busy for Mary to engage in any more small talk, the next two hours being a constant barrage of taking orders and filling plates. Everyone was a friend, most ordering the same thing day after day. Often Mary would see regular customers walking up the street and she would have their food waiting when they walked in the front door. Only once did her perfect system fail. A kindly regular customer oiled the creaky old hinges on the diner's front door. Mary couldn't hear people coming in and it threw her rhythm into a tailspin. She wiped the oil from the hinge pins and the familiar squeak returned.

Life had settled into a very regular, boring routine for Mary. The diner took many of her hours, her church took what remained. No changes, no deviation from procedures. This life was exactly what Mary Johnson wanted. Ruby had never once returned to work, not even to visit with the regulars or to see if Mary was running the diner as she wanted. Mary had seen her only once after he visit with Sheriff Jenkins. She had stopped by Ruby's home to ask for permission to paint the diner and replace the ancient refrigerator. Years of sunshine and smoke filled air had changed the bright colors to a dull, dirty looking finish, and the old refrigerator often did not keep anything cold. The changes would be expensive, but Mary felt they were necessary.

She had dropped the large doorknocker and cringed a bit as the hollow boom sounded inside the house. After what seemed like an eternity Mary shrugged and walked slowly down the walkway. Reaching the cracked sidewalk, she began retracing her steps to the diner. Almost a hundred yards from Ruby's door she heard someone yell "Hey." Looking over her shoulder, she saw Ruby standing in her doorway, pointing a finger at Mary like a prosecutor to a hostile witness. "What do you want" Ruby had shouted.

Mary walked back to her and smiled. "Good afternoon Ruby. How have you been?"

"Is that all you wanted?" the old woman snapped. "You could have asked one of those wag tongued big mouths from town and got the answer to that one. The doctor took away my cigarettes and I might just as well be dead, that's how I'm doing." She coughed a low, rattling wet sound as if to emphasize her position and slammed the door shut.

Mary rolled her eyes and whistled softly. She dropped the door knocker and listened to the boom, this time waiting until the door opened again.

"Now what do you want" Ruby snapped.

"I want your permission to paint the diner and buy a new refrigerator" Mary said.

She was about to list the reasons why that was the right thing to do when Ruby interrupted. "Listen to me. You run the diner, not me. Mess things up and you're out on your ear. Do whatever you think will help and don't bother me with details. Stan Kenton will tell me if the bank account starts going down."

Mary had been too shocked to speak, so she stood dumbly on the top step and stared at her employer. Ruby stared back, coughing and hacking from time to time which at least broke the total silence.

"By the way" Ruby finally snapped, "I'm going to Florida so I can escape this blasted cold. Stan will call me if necessary, just see him if you've got any problems. Now get off my porch." The door slammed closed with sufficient force to cause the door knocker to bang on its own initiative.

The entire conversation was too amusing to be insulting, so Mary suppressed a smile and walked home. She made changes, bought equipment and redecorated whenever she thought it prudent, and business continued to increase. She ordered what she needed and directed the bills to Stan Kenton at the bank.

Mary realized she was reminiscing as she worked, mechanically fixing food orders with half her conscious mind while the other half rambled. She noticed that Ed was sitting at a nearby table with a glass of orange juice, and Mary blushed as she realized he was watching her every move. "Have you been here all morning?" she asked, using a hand engulfed in soap bubbles to carefully scratch the end of her nose. Satisfying the itch, she still breathed some bubbles up her nostrils. They popped soundlessly and caused her to sneeze violently, now spraying soap bubbles into the air around her head.

Sheriff Jenkins chuckled at the sight, covering his mouth with a big hand in a futile effort to hide his mirth. "I've been here all morning" he said. "I just wasn't in the mood to get involved with the day, so I decided to just sit right here and watch you."

Mary blushed a deeper crimson. He looked and sounded exactly like her brother Jeff when he laughed and talked at the same time. She felt a strange combination of love and sadness, both emotions threatening to make her cry, so she shook her head and plunged her hands back into the dishwater. Uncomfortable because he continued to sit in silence and watch her work, Mary hurried to finish the work.

Sheriff Jenkins heaved a sigh of resolve and banged his now empty glass on the top of the table. "Mary, I want to ask you something. We've known each other for a number of years now, and I'm a little bit older than you and all, but I was wondering something." His ears burned red with embarrassment as he talked and his big hands twirled the glass with increasing speed on the top of the table.

Her heart started pounding like a bass drum in a parade, and Mary leaned forward as if to grasp his words in her hands. When she tried to speak nothing came out so she swallowed and tried again. "Yes Ed, what do you want to ask me."

"Well, I was wondering if maybe you, I mean we, well maybe some time..."

The diner's door flew open, a breathless Stan Kenton running as fast as his overweight body would take him. His face glowed red as a fireplace coal, and he halted in front of the counter gasping for breath. Leaning on a stool and waving first at Mary and then Sheriff Jenkins, he tried to speak but failed at each attempt. Mary drew a glass of water which she sat in front of Stan, he acknowledging her kindness with a nod and then splashed some on his face.

"Stan, do you want me to get the doctor?" Sheriff

Jenkins asked, obviously worried about his friend.

"No, no. Alright. I'm okay" he gasped and finally sank down on a stool at the counter. He looked at Mary and motioned her closer. When she leaned over her side of the counter he took several deep breaths and finally spoke in his usual clear voice. "Mary, have you ever heard of Carpenter and Reece Investments from Cincinnati?"

"No, I don't guess that I have" she said with a small shake of her head. "What is this all about Stan?"

He drank half the water in the glass in one large gulp before answering. "They are, without a doubt, the number one financial planning company in the state. Presidents of large corporations, all the political party leaders on both sides, and just about anybody else with clout uses them. They turn away more people than they take."

"What's all that got to do with me Stan" Mary asked, a puzzled frown on her face.

"Mary, I've got some news" Stan said. He reached out and took her left hand in both of his own. "Ruby passed away yesterday in Florida."

Mary's knees turned to jelly and she thought she might fall down. Stan increased his grip on her hand and that gave her the strength to remain upright. "This is awful" she said, "but I hardly knew her. I worked for her all these years and only spoke to her a couple of times. I'm ashamed to say I feel more fear for my future than I do grief for Ruby."

"That's understandable my dear" Stan reassured. "Ruby didn't really have any friends, she was overall just too darn cantankerous. But that's not the whole of it. I've got Todd Carpenter himself in my office. He's the one who told me about Ruby, and then he says he's got business to conduct with you."

Mary pulled back, the thought of her father with the Barlow knife sticking out of him and the long arm of the justice reaching for her throat made the old fear arise. "Why would he have any business with me?" she asked, her voice trembling slightly.

"I don't know" Stan said. "All I can tell you is the last time Todd Carpenter came to see someone instead of expecting them to come to him was when the Governor invited him to the mansion for a working lunch. Mr. Carpenter just doesn't do business outside his office. Come on, I'll take you to him."

Mary looked toward Ed for support, overwhelmed at the unexpected change in events.

"Come on" the sheriff said in answer to her look. He pushed to his feet and started for the door. "I'll go with you and we'll see what this fellow's got to say."

"I don't know" Stan said nervously, "Mr. Carpenter didn't say that anyone else could be there."

"Well, if Ed isn't there then I'm afraid Mr. Carpenter took a drive this morning for pure pleasure" Mary said, hoping the firmness in her tone was real and not imagined.

"Fine, I guess if that's the way it has to be that's what you can tell him" Stan said, with an emphasis on the word you.

The walk to the bank was made in silence, Stan hurrying with a worried frown on his face and pausing several times to impatiently wait as Mary and Sheriff Jenkins caught up with him. Mary felt the early morning sun, already hot as it traveled higher into the sky, and felt a bit faint. She stiffened her arms and legs to make them feel stronger and willed her head to clear.

When they entered the bank the air felt cooler but only for a moment. Perspiration rolled down her back and sides, soaking her white blouse. Stan Kenton was again gasping for breath but continued to hurry them toward his office. Sheriff Jenkins was impassive and appeared to be cool despite the humid air.

A tall, slender man in a Brooks Brothers suit and spit shined Florsheim's stood at the window behind Stan Kenton's desk. He was intently studying a pidgin standing on the ledge, tapping at the window with his index finger as the bird tapped in return with its beak on the other side of the glass. He turned as they entered the office, Stan and Mary still sweating, the sheriff still cool and collected, and he flashed a warm, trust me I'm an expert, smile. The man's teeth were straight and even, white as polished ivory, and almost blinded Mary in their contrast to his sun browned skin. Salt and pepper black hair with just the right amount of gray mixed in gave him a mature yet not old look.

"Hello, I'm Todd Carpenter" he said in a low yet rich voice. His eyes sparkled as he smiled, crow's feet at the corner of each eye crinkling in unison as if they were choreographed. He held out a smooth hand that gripped firm when Mary shook it, and she noticed his nails were freshly manicured with a shiny transparent clear coat of polish on each. "You must be Mary. I feel I know you even though we've never met."

"Why would you know Mary?" Sheriff Jenkins asked, his usual friendly face now guarded and even somewhat menacing.

"You must be Ed Jenkins" Todd Carpenter said instead of answering his question. "Ruby told me a lot about you too, although I must admit you're a bit easier to spot in that uniform." He smiled even broader, his capped teeth seeming to be showing off by themselves. "I can't say I've looked forward to meeting both of you, since our getting together is a result of Ruby's passing, but I must admit I've always wanted to add faces to your names. You're both exactly as I would have pictured."

"Why are you here Mr. Carpenter" Mary asked. She was grateful when her voice did not quiver.

"Ruby asked me to come here before she died" he said. "I owe her a great deal and so I promised I would stop here first before going on to Florida and arranging for her burial." He smiled again at their questioning looks and then went on. "When I was just a boy, I was traveling with my mother and father and we were hit by a semi truck just outside of the city limits here in Brecksville. My parents were unconscious and I was too young and scared to get out of the car myself."

He paused a moment, as if the memory were too much to handle, then went on. "Our car started to burn, I suppose the gas tank ruptured and spilled onto the hot tail pipe. I remember how hot I was and seeing the flames all around me. Suddenly out of nowhere a woman was pulling at the door on my mother's side. It was stuck and she was cursing like a sailor, I remember that like it was yesterday. I also remember seeing the paint peeling on the car, so I knew it was actually hotter outside than in.

"She actually tore the door off the car, like Superman coming to the rescue. It sounded like a big thick top of a can coming off without an opener. Then she pulled my mother out and dragged her away from the fire, at least to the point when other people that were too afraid to get closer could take over. Then she climbed in and pulled father from behind the steering wheel, dragged him across the seat, and carried him away from the fire. He was a big man too, I'd guess maybe two twenty or so."

Carpenter blinked twice, forced his eyes on his audience for a moment, then continued with his story. "I remember flames all around me then. I was so hot my skin started bubbling and I was close to bursting into flames. Ruby came to the car one more time, her hair was smoking now, and reached across the seat. She actually scared me worse than the fire. She was all black from soot and being burned, and with the smoke pouring off her hair she looked like some kind of demon from a nightmare.

"I put my head down because I was scared and didn't want to look at her, and do you know what she did?" She grabbed the back of my neck like a dog does her pups and snatched me over the seat and out the door in one motion. She actually carried me by pinching the skin on my neck. The car exploded and the blast knocked us ten feet through the air and we both landed in the back of a pickup truck.

The guy who owned the truck just started it up and took us both to the hospital."

Carpenter shrugged and lifted an eyebrow. "I owe my life to that woman. She damaged her lungs and still smoked, I'm sure that shortened her life too. Anyway, I've done pretty well with investment advice, and a number of years ago Ruby asked me to help her manage her assets. That included administering her estate, so here I am today."

Mary was too caught up in his tale to be frightened anymore, and asked the question that remained unanswered. "How did your parents come out of the accident?"

He smiled at her and nodded. "I would have guessed you would ask from what Ruby told me about you. They were fine. Both recovered fully and actually live in Florida not too far from Ruby. They're taking care of some of the arrangements until I get there."

"But I still don't know why you wanted to see me" Mary asked. "Are you closing the diner?"

Carpenter shook his head. "No, unless you choose to close it Mary."

"What do you mean if I choose to" she asked, confusion showing in a frown.

"Mary, what did Ruby pay you to work in the diner all these years" Carpenter asked.

Mary blushed, not comfortable talking about her meager existence, but supposing she had to answer the man's question. "Well, I ate all the food from the diner I wanted, I stayed for free in the room at the rear of the building, and I got my clothes from Mr. Flannery at his store. He told me I had an open account and Ruby would tell him if I spent too much."

"Didn't you receive any pay?" Sheriff Jenkins asked incredulously. She was such a closed person he never talked about such things with her, yet he never noticed that she didn't seem to spend any money.

"Well, I would get ten dollars in the mail each month" she said, eyes downcast in embarrassment. "It was always a ten dollar bill. I just gave most of it to the church because I didn't really need anything."

Carpenter looked at her with a bemused expression. "Didn't you ever think you should be getting a decent wage for running the diner?" he asked.

"Mr. Carpenter, I was so grateful to have a normal life I was afraid to ask for anything. I don't know what's fair or not, but I do know I didn't want to go back to my old life. In fact that's why I'm scared to death right now that you're going to close the diner. I guess it's the most important thing in my life, or at least it lets me have a life."

Carpenter nodded his head, then walked to the edge of Stan Kenton's desk. He lifted one long leg and draped it across the corner of the highly polished wood and leaned forward in the manner of a confidant. "First of all, just so you'll know all of the facts, there was no account at the general store. Whatever Flannery was giving you was strictly on his own. Ruby has always been pretty tight with a dollar, and she probably figured you would ask if you needed help."

"Then Fred Flannery" Mary began, a puzzled look on her face.

"Fred Flannery is a sentimental soft touch" Stan Kenton inserted. "He would give his last dime to someone who needed it less than himself, which is pretty much what the loveable old fool has done too often. He's in debt to the point that he's going to lose his store, and it's all because he gives too much away."

"But that's not why I'm here" Carpenter said, a bit irritated by being sidetracked. "Ruby has no family, and besides my family I don't think she has any friends. Heaven only knows she could be pretty crusty with people."

"Amen to that" Stan Kenton said. "She once closed her account here because we gave away toasters to new depositors. She said if we had money to throw away on giveaways we should have lowered the fees on her checking account. I swear she drove twenty minutes to Rawlings each day to do her banking. She stuck to her guns for over a year until we finally stopped giving away toasters. Ruby always believed she caused us to stop the promotion, although the truth was it just ran its course. I sure would never have said otherwise though, since at least she brought her business back to town."

"Moving on" Carpenter almost barked, withering Stan with a look, "Ruby wanted me to settle her affairs quickly and without fanfare. That's where you come in Mary."

"I still don't understand Mr. Carpenter" Mary said.

"Please, call me Todd" he said warmly.

Stan Kenton nearly fell from his chair at the offer of familiarity to a restaurant manager while he, president of a bank, was never offered the same courtesy.

"Very well Todd" Mary said, "but I still don't understand. The few times I talked to Ruby, she was downright nasty and rude to me. Unless she wanted you to throw me out on my ear yourself, I can't imagine why I would be on your agenda."

"Ruby being rude was her way" Carpenter said. "She took great pride in not permitting anyone to know how she felt about them. You see Mary, Ruby admired you more than anyone she knew. You took the diner way beyond her abilities and she knew it. I asked her why she didn't tell you that herself and she told me she couldn't. When you've been the way you are all your life it's hard to change."

"I certainly understand that" Mary agreed.

"Now, again coming back to the reason for my visit." Carpenter opened a saddle leather briefcase with the initials TC on the front in gold. He pulled out a notepad and several official looking documents, including one which said Last Will and Testament across the top. "Ruby owned the diner and her house, of which neither has a mortgage, plus I've made investments for her over the years that equal a considerable amount of money. Her will instructs me, and I've taken the liberty of drawing up the appropriate documents, to sign all of her earthly possessions to one Mary Johnson, currently manager of Ruby's Diner."

The office was silent as a tomb, Stan Kenton having drawn a breath which he now held, and Sheriff Jenkins remained as impassive as ever. Carpenter was looking at the legal documents one last time, needlessly checking for the fifth or sixth time their accuracy, and Mary had fainted. She sat in her chair, chin resting on her chest as if asleep, and no one noticed.

Stan Kenton finally expelled his breath in a whoosh a bare instant before he passed out himself, and this seemed to awaken the entire room. The sheriff leaped to Mary's side, patting her hand as she slowly recovered and looked about in confusion. Todd Carpenter scowled as he looked up and then sat upright in surprise.

"Get her a glass of water" Sheriff Jenkins barked at Stan Kenton, who hurried from the room to comply. "Mary, are you alright? Do you need a doctor?"

"No, I'm fine" she said, "I just got a bit overwhelmed I guess. I mean how can I take all of Ruby's things? I'm not a relative or anything, in fact I'm not even a friend."

"I'm afraid that doesn't matter" Carpenter said. "When there's no one to contest a will, which in this case there isn't, it's pretty much a cut and dried affair. Oh, some of the final transfers will actually take a couple of months, but anything you need in the meantime can be handled by the bank with a letter of credit."

"Absolutely" Stan Kenton said as he hurried a paper cup of water to Mary's side. "Anything she needs I'll handle personally."

"I don't know" Mary said, gratefully drinking the water. "Me owning the diner and a house? I can't imagine that much wealth."

Todd Carpenter chuckled. "Mary, the diner and house are a mere drop in the bucket. With your holdings in stock and savings you could buy ten diners and houses."

She felt faint again, so she waved a hand in front of her flushed face. "I don't know how to handle all of this."

"That's why we're all here" Carpenter soothed. "If you wish I'll maintain your investments and Stan can handle your banking day to day needs. I'm sure our friend the sheriff here will make sure we treat you fairly and handle your money wisely" he added with a smile.

"When can I use the money" Mary asked, suddenly sitting straight in her chair.

"Just as soon as you sign these forms" Carpenter said. "You might want someone to look them over for you to make sure everything is in order" he added as he spread the documents in a precise pattern on the desk.

"I think I can trust you Mr. Carpenter, I mean Todd" Mary answered. She picked up the pen and began signing, then glanced at Stan Kenton. "Stan, would you please get Fred Flannery's note and show the balance due to Todd?"

"Well, I'm not sure if it's appropriate to make public another customer's debt level" Stan Kenton blustered.

Mary signed the last form with a bit of a flourish before she turned to the flustered banker. "Stan, you already told us Fred is about to lose his store. If you'll just do as I ask I promise I won't be angry when you tell everyone in town that I inherited Ruby's money and, which is probably even a bigger news item, that my last name is Johnson as Todd already said."

"Well, I mean, well, very well." Stan Kenton cleared his throat and ran a finger around his shirt collar as if that would remove some of the red in his cheeks. He hurried from the room with a nervous glance over his shoulder.

Todd Carpenter shook his head in amazement and disgust as he stared at the retreating banker. He turned his attention to Mary, putting his index finger beside his long, straight nose like a handsome, thin Santa Claus in a suit. He winked at Mary and said, "I do believe you'll handle yourself and this windfall quite well young lady. And I do apologize that I used your last name. It never occurred to me that you kept that to yourself."

"That's alright" Mary said with a smile. "May I ask, how did you know my last name?"

"I'm the best in the business because I know everything" Carpenter said as he slid a thumb and forefinger along a razor sharp crease in his trousers. "You're going to pay off Flannery's debt aren't you" he said, changing the subject.

"Will I have enough money to do that?" she asked.

"I can't imagine that you wouldn't" he said. "You're not going to be limitlessly wealthy, but this is a fair amount of money, plus you also will have income from the diner. I would, however, suggest that you let me analyze the value of the store before you buy into it as a partner. Because Flannery is obviously desperate I can probably get you controlling interest."

Stan Kenton came bursting in with a folder filled with loan documents. He opened the cover and pointed to a figure on the top page circled in red. "This is what Fred owes" he wheezed. "He's got two weeks before we close the store."

"Do I have enough to pay the debt?" Mary asked.

Carpenter whistled softly. "This is a lot more than I would have expected. I would roughly say this is a third of your stocks and bonds Mary. I wouldn't advise buying in for this much, especially since the store hasn't been modernized for years. A strong competitor would put him under."

"Todd, I think that's good advice" Mary said. "I don't think I want to own a general store, all or part. That's Fred's life and he should have it."

Stan Kenton almost raised his hand as if to ask for permission to speak. "Well, ah, Mary, you see he won't own it anyway in two more weeks."

"Oh yes he will" Mary said, smiling and rising to

her feet. "Todd, please transfer enough money to pay the note. I'll sign whatever paperwork is necessary."

"Then you are buying in" Carpenter said, obviously a bit confused.

Mary glanced at Sheriff Jenkins who had moved to the door and held it open for her. He had a large, knowing smile on his face. She smiled back at him and walked to the doorway, stopping just before her exit and turning to the astonished banker and investment councilor. "All I'm doing gentlemen, is paying my bill for clothing and incidentals over the years."

"But Mary" Stan Kenton said, scratching his head in amazement, "you wouldn't spend this much in Flannery's for a hundred years."

"Stan, all I know is those incidentals add up" Mary said and, taking Sheriff Jenkins by the arm, they walked out together.

THIRTEEN

Mary held a large cardboard sign, a roll of masking tape, and a pair of scissors. Sheriff Jenkins and Fred Flannery stood at her side to lend encouragement more than help. She centered the cardboard on the inside of the large front window of the diner. The lettering was bold and legible, printed in neat block letters in perfectly straight lines. It read,

> RUBY'S WILL BE CLOSED
> FOR ONE WEEK
> FIRST DAY BACK, FREE MEALS

"I don't agree with the giveaway" Sheriff Jenkins commented when, after the sign was in place, they went outside and looked at her handiwork from the sidewalk. "These people love you Mary. One week away will not cause anyone to take their business elsewhere."

"I know, but I want to give something back for all the years of patronage" Mary said. "I feel like I owe that."

"You've already given us what we paid for" Fred Flannery said. "You fill a plate for the money, which is not only fair but it's sensible."

Mary smiled and patted his arm. "And look who's talking about charging a fair price for something, Mr. give his last penny to the poor."

Fred Flannery blushed and smiled shyly in return. "Aw, I just knew that some day you could pay off all my debts so I was staying on your good side."

The three friends laughed and walked toward the

sheriff's office. A flowered canvas bag sat on a bench positioned under the sheriff's window like a dog patiently waiting for its owner. The trio stopped by a bus stop sign with a sleek greyhound on top and Mary sat primly on the front edge of the bench. Fred Flannery positioned himself beside her, staring down the narrow city street as if he could will the bus into view. The sheriff placed a foot on the arm rest of the bench, then crossed his arms and rested them on his raised knee.

"I really wish you would reconsider this trip" Sheriff Jenkins said, a worried frown on his face.

"Ed, I've just got to know what happened to my father" Mary replied, squinting from the sun as she looked up at him. "Besides, I made a promise to Myra years ago that I would help her if I was able, and for goodness sakes I certainly am in a position to do just that."

"You don't even know if she needs your help" he argued, moving to position himself between Mary and the sun. His head caused a shadow to fall across her eyes, reducing the glare. "Plus, I could run some interference and see if there's anything out there concerning your father."

"Thanks" she said, referring to his shadow from the sun. Then she said, "I won't have you risking your badge for me. If anyone found out you knew I was wanted and did nothing, well I won't have that on my shoulders. I'm going to Myra first, and she may be able to tell me what happened. If not, I'll look into it myself. It's time I knew and had some answers. I need to put it behind me, no matter what the result."

"Well, I may understand it but I don't have to like it" Sheriff Jenkins said and cocked his hat back on his head. You only protected yourself, and dragging anything up is just not necessary."

"But it is for me" she said, and gently laid her hand on his forearm.

"If anything does come of it Mary, I'll sell the store and hire the best lawyers in the State" Fred Flannery said.

He knew her background, having become one of her closest friends after she helped him with his debts. Flannery was a good friend to most everyone, but with Mary he was fiercely loyal.

"I don't think we have anything to be concerned with" Mary said with false confidence, "but it is nice to have friends like the two of you." She wiped a tear from the corner of her eye and said, "I never knew people cared about each other. Oh, I knew there was a lot of pretending by various people, but I mean true friendships. No matter what happens from here, I'll always have the two of you. Nothing can take that away from me."

Fred Flannery blushed with pleasure and Sheriff Jenkins smiled and winked. They fell quiet for a time, talked out and simply not having more to say. Mary closed her eyes and drank in the pleasant sounds of the town where she had learned what the word security meant. Birds sang happily in the trees lining the main street, breezes whistled around corners of buildings in familiar patterns, and Mary felt the peace in their community cover Brecksville like a warm blanket in the winter.

The sun fell on her face again, the warmth of it touching her cheek like a soft hand, also letting her know that Sheriff Jenkins had moved his shadow. She opened her eyes reluctantly, not anxious to break the spell which had come over her. He was moving her bag to the ground to make room on the bench for a seat beside her. Settling on the sturdy old bench, his gun belt creaking as the leather shifted position, he tentatively reached out and took Mary's hand in his, holding it as gently as if it were a delicate flower.

Fred Flannery looked at them for a moment and then smiled. He cleared his throat and stretched his arms over his head, yawning like a bored party guest. "You know, I'd better get back to the store" he said. "I'm having a sale on light bulbs and when Martha is working the register she sometimes forgets to ring the sale price. I can't afford to have customer's think I'm cheating them you know, I could lose business." He touched Mary's shoulder and sighed. "If you don't mind I'll let Ed see you off."

Mary stood and threw her arms around her friend. "Of course I don't mind Fred. I'll see you in a week, okay?"

"That's a deal" he said as he returned her hug. "Just promise you'll call if you have any trouble or need help."

"I promise. Now you behave while I'm gone."

"That's a promise too" he said as he pulled away. With a wave he hurried across the street toward his store.

Mary held her hand palm out just above her head as a gesture of good-bye and held her position until Fred Flannery reached the entrance of his store. When he turned, waved again and went inside, Mary dropped her arm and sat again by the sheriff. "He is such a dear man" she said, still looking toward the store.

"They don't come any better" Sheriff Jenkins agreed. He folded his hands in his lap, twisting his fingers nervously in a meaningless pattern. His head was lowered and he seemed to be studying the nervous fingers. After a few moments he spoke, slowly and deliberately. "Mary, I want to tell you something that I've been carrying around in my heart for some time now, and with you going away, even if it is only for a week, I want to say it while I have the courage."

Shifting slightly to look at him more comfortably, Mary frowned with concern and placed her hand over his twisting fingers which immediately became still. "Ed, I would hope you could say anything to me" she said softly. "You are the very first true friend I have ever had, and I would always want us to talk about anything."

Turning his hands over, he again held her hand in his, rubbing his left thumb gently over her knuckle. "I know I'm older than you" he began, pausing to take a deep breath before going on. "When you first came here you were a scared kid escaping from a brutal life and I wanted to see you have a chance. Then, you grew up. I mean you physically grew. You've always been very mature, I guess your circumstances forced that."

He looked up now, their eyes locking like two beams connected them. "Over the years as I got to know you, I realized that you were exactly the person I always thought of when I asked myself who would be my life's partner. I guess what I'm saying is I've fallen in love with you." He dropped his eyes again and stared at her hand. "I know I'm too old and all, but I feel the way I do and I wanted to tell you."

Mary looked down the street as if willing the bus to appear and save her from this conversation. The black surface stretched to the horizon and not even a pedestrian or a bicycle could be seen. She sighed in resignation and looked at the sheriff. Mary almost flinched at the look of hope she saw, mixed with fear.

"Ed, you are beyond a doubt the best man I have ever known. If everyone were like you, well, my life would be very different than it is today. The problem is, this is my life. The things that have happened to me happened. Nothing can change that."

Mary stood and began to nervously pace back and forth in front of the bench. She put one hand on her chin as if to help support the weight of her head, unconsciously chewing on a fingernail. Then she plopped down on the bench and grabbed his hands with her own, tears springing to the corners of her eyes like a leaky faucet. "Ed, my dear Ed, I'm not sure I could ever have a normal relationship with a man. The only way I knew any man as a girl was through pain and fear. I want to know what it's like to love and be loved the right way, but I'm afraid."

"Mary, I would never hurt you for anything in the world" Sheriff Jenkins said in a whisper.

"I know that" she answered, squeezing his hands, "but even though I know in my heart you aren't like the others I can't move past my fear. It's like being afraid of high places. The fear is stupid and irrational, but it's still real fear. As wrong as it is, it's still there."

"So what do we do?" he asked, looking helpless for the first time since Mary had known him.

"I can only say I need time" she replied sadly. "I don't know if I will ever change Ed, and that's the total truth, but I am sure that I'm not able to promise anything, at least not now. I wouldn't want you to wait for me to change though, because that isn't fair to you."

"Mary, I've been waiting for you all my life, so I don't see how more time could make any difference. After all, what else do I have to do?" He smiled and winked at her, the old Ed Jenkins back again.

"Well, I certainly don't see what you're waiting for" Mary said with a small shrug. "I'm just a beat up girl who owns a diner."

"What more could a man ask for" he said, chuckling as she smiled and blushed. "You know, I think it's the dish pan hands that attracted me more than anything."

Grateful that he dropped the serious attitude, Mary brightened and changed the subject. "I think I'll sell Ruby's house. I go over there almost every day and walk around, but I just can't feel comfortable. It's so big and dark, and everything smells like smoke."

"You could redecorate. New carpeting, fresh paint, maybe even new draperies would make the place like new, and windows open might air the old place out" he said.

"I don't know if anything would help" she said. "It's just so big and empty, kind of like a small country of its own. Maybe since I lived in that small cabin, then in a mobile home, and now my little room in the diner, that taught me to like things closed in."

"Or maybe smaller feels more secure" Sheriff Jenkins said, "like being held in someone's arms."

"That could be Dr. Freud" she agreed. "Whatever the reason, that house is not for me. I guess I can decide what to do when I come home."

"There certainly is no hurry, and I doubt anyone will bother it even though it's empty. The school kids will eventually toss rocks through the windows if it stays vacant too long, but that wouldn't happen until someone started a rumor about the place being haunted."

"Actually, that might be fun" Mary said, sitting straighter in anticipation of the stunt. "I could take a lantern from one room to another late at night, then snuff it out when anyone came near. We would have this little town jumping like firecrackers."

"What do you mean we" Sheriff Jenkins replied. "I can just see it now, the local sheriff getting caught helping his crazy friend scare the locals half to death." He scratched his chin and added, "Although, it would be a devil of a lot of fun wouldn't it."

"Oh, just stop" she laughed. "For goodness sakes it's getting so I can talk you into anything."

Suddenly serious again he shook his head. "You know, you're right Mary. I would do just about anything for you."

"Now don't go getting somber again" Mary demanded. "Let's just enjoy each other's friendship for now like we agreed."

"You're right" he said, slapping his hand on his thigh, "besides, here comes your bus." It grew from a speck in the distance to a roaring monolith which seemed to go from full speed to a sudden stop precisely at the edge of the bus stop.

The greyhound dog painted on the side of the bus seemed to be panting as the engine idled, exhaust fumes swirling about like wind swept leaves in the early fall. Several people looked out open windows on the bus like prisoners wishing they could step off and join people who were not compelled to race across the country, but they remained immobile in their seats and frowned with envy as they waited. A small boy hung half way out a window, dangerously close to squirting out of the bus like a seed from a watermelon, but his mother grabbed the back of his trousers and snatched him back inside. The boy wailed like a trapped animal deep in the belly of the bus.

Sheriff Jenkins insisted on putting her bag into the undercarriage of the bus himself, ignoring the grumbles from the driver about "Union rules" and "Let me do my job." The sheriff walked with Mary to the three steps that led into the Greyhound, then he quickly swept her into his arms and kissed her. She shuddered as his cool lops touched hers, not sure if what she felt were fear or pleasure. Quickly he stepped away and held one hand in the air as a goodbye.

"Call me if you need anything or if there's trouble" he said. "I'll be there at a moment's notice."

"I'll be fine" Mary said, holding her hand aloft and giving him a soft smile. She ran up the steps of the bus, the door snapping shut almost on her heel as the driver hurried to get underway. The bus moved forward as she headed for a seat, so Mary rushed to the long bench style seat at the rear of the bus.

The sheriff was standing in the middle of the street, his hand still raised as if he could reach out and pull her back to him. Mary waved again and then pulled her hand to her mouth. She could still feel the outline of his lips on her face, the stubble of his beard leaving a prickly feeling on her upper lip.

She turned in the seat when she couldn't see him any longer, his shape disappearing from her vision after they crested a hill. She wondered how long he stayed in the street looking after the bus, and Mary felt an uneasiness in her stomach. She smiled to herself, running her index finger around her lips, and realized that she already missed him.

FOURTEEN

The ride was long and very boring. Mary discovered that, despite her anxiety concerning the end of the trip, she still was drawn into sleep. With a constant side to side motion she felt rocked like a baby, the low rumble of the bus engine sounding like a low song of comfort.

Mary awoke with a start as the Greyhound pulled to a stop in a small parking lot covered with pea gravel. The driver yelled "Lunch stop. Be on the bus in precisely thirty minutes please. There will be no boarding call or seat checks folks. I have a very reliable Timex which will be our official time piece. If you're interested I have exactly," he paused to consult his left wrist, "exactly eleven forty seven. Please be back on the coach in plenty of time."

The driver pulled on the shiny chrome handle on the end of a black rod which opened the bus door. The passengers had lined up like cattle in a slaughter house chute as he barked his instructions, which resulted in a mini trampling as they bolted out the door. Experienced travelers were well aware that very little time could be wasted if they were to order food, wait for it to be cooked, gulp it down, and then be securely back in their seat before the huge metal hound returned to its endless chase of the rabbit. The first people inside would be seated and served with no problem. The hapless souls who were last might end up with indigestion, have no time to eat at all, or even worse could find themselves stranded. The latter problem meant waiting for the next bus, which typically would come the following day.

Mary watched the pushing and shoving almost absentmindedly from her rear seat, waiting patiently as the people flowed out the door. A young woman and three small children waited in their seats as well, finally standing when the bus emptied. Mary did not move until they had exited. Her head rang with the false echo of sound from the noisy bus.

Slowly she walked down the aisle, her shoes kicking an occasional candy wrapper, a discarded newspaper, and other trash strewn throughout the bus. The travelers were inside the small restaurant as she stepped down onto the gravel drive, a quiet crunch sounding as she walked toward the shabby looking eatery. The place reminded her of the restaurant where Sharon had worked so many years ago. The memory was suddenly so vivid it stopped her in midstride, the thought of a man's torn face, courtesy of her father, flashing in her mind.

The sound of children crying pulled Mary's attention to the side of the small restaurant, the tears reminding her, as it always did, of her brothers being mistreated by Ray Don. The young woman with the three children was looking into a large garbage can just outside the kitchen door. The children were identical triplets, delicate little girls wearing mismatched, shabby clothes, but beautiful despite their tear stained faces. Each had shoulder length blonde curly hair that glistened like spun gold in the sunlight. Their mother, herself a strikingly beautiful blonde wearing a dark blue dress patched and sewn in several places, was picking scraps of sandwiches and steak bones with a small amount of meat on them out of the garbage. She spoke in slow, soothing tones to the children as they looked at the bits of food as it was placed on a piece of newspaper. Mary walked slowly toward them, drawn like a magnet to the little drama. The group didn't seem to notice her, so she stopped a short distance away and listened to what they said.

"I don't want to eat garbage Mama" one triplet said

through her tears.

"Can't we eat some real food?" the next little girl asked, not crying anymore.

"Yea, real food Mama" the last triplet added, also blubbering through tears.

"I'm sorry girls, we just don't have any more money" their mother soothed, digging deeper into the garbage can. "We've got to have food, and without money this is the only choice we've got."

Without thinking Mary blurted out, "No, that's not your only choice at all."

The little group froze in place as if they were statues, heads turned toward Mary in a combination of fear and shame. Suddenly, the little girls moved as if one unit to hide behind their mother's skirts. "Are we doing something wrong?" the woman asked, spreading her legs a bit wider to create a larger barrier for the children to take refuge, like a hen ruffling her feathers in defense of her chicks.

Mary smiled, shaking her head slowly and spreading her hands out, palms up, to demonstrate a nonthreatening attitude. "Of course not, you're just doing what you have to do for your children. I overheard you quite by accident, and although I don't want to intrude, I would like to offer some help if you don't mind."

The woman relaxed just the slightest bit, her protective guard still raised but sensing this may be the opportunity for some welcome relief. "If you have any way to help me not feed my kids garbage, then I certainly want to hear about it" she said, the bitterness in her voice impossible to hide.

"Give me just a moment" Mary said and stepped to the kitchen door. She peered through the screen door, the inside door having been blocked open to let the heat from the ovens and stoves escape, and looked around. The small work area was a mess with piles of empty boxes and cans stacked everywhere. Five men were crammed into the small space, all moving at breakneck speed and shouting at each other.

With amazing accuracy food was piled on plates, matched with a light blue order slip that hung from a round metal wheel, and the slip was placed under the edge of the plate. A bell with a metal striker on its top was slapped as each plate hit the countertop, the cook who completed the task yelling "Pickup" in the general direction of a server. The process was all so fast the bell seldom stopped its vibration before it was sounded again.

Mary quickly assessed the five men, picking out one who she determined was in charge of the crew. Opening the screen door she stepped into the kitchen, the familiar smells, sounds and heat washing over her like an old friend. Touching the man's shoulder, she smiled and waved a friendly little greeting as he jumped in surprise and turned to face her.

"Hey, you can't be in here" he growled, brandishing a long handled spatula like a weapon.

"I think you're going to want to talk to me" Mary said, shouting over the din. "My conversation involves money."

Instantly she had his attention. He nodded toward the screen door and said, "Let's step outside for a minute and we'll talk."

Mary nodded and backed out of the kitchen, the cook matching her movements with his own. He had lowered the spatula but still carried it in his hand, just in case there was trouble. The mother and her three girls now stood a short distance away, watching Mary and the cook with curious stares.

"Okay lady, what you got" he asked, glancing over his shoulder into the bustling kitchen. His cook's whites were threadbare and discolored, with faded patterns of stains only partially washed out despite hundreds of washings. His face was flushed from the heat but despite the color in his cheeks his eyes still looked tired and troubled. Already regretting the time he was taking with this woman, he thought about his wife and their four children. He had to get back to work fast, because the last thing he could afford to do was lose his job. "I only got a second, so please talk fast okay?" he said, looking again over his shoulder. One of the men inside was glancing out with an irritated look on his face.

"I'll be brief" Mary said, all business. "How much do you get paid for a week's work" she asked.

The man was obviously stunned. He opened and closed his mouth twice, then took one step to the rear and stared at Mary. He raised the spatula, this time using it like a pointer instead of a weapon. He closed one eye, turned his lips up on one side to form a sideways grin, paused for a full five seconds, then dropped his arms to his sides. "Forty bucks a week" he blurted out, as if after thinking it over he had made a 'oh, what the heck, let's see where this goes' decision.

Mary opened the snap on her hand bag, pulled open the leather top, and reached inside while peering in like a dentist working on a stubborn tooth. Instead of extracting an incisor she pulled out a fifty dollar bill. The cook's eyes widened as he saw over a week's pay in her hand. That represented school clothes for his kids with enough left over to buy his wife that red and black checkered table cloth she had been dreaming about and at least two new pair of cook's whites for him. With an extreme effort he raised his eyes from the smooth green bill to look at Mary's face. He sucked in his breath hard to prevent the hint of drool which was about to appear on his lower lip. Mary held the fifty with the thumb and index finger of both hands on the outer edges of the bill, lifting her arms to display the prize at shoulder level.

"Quite simply" she began, snapping the bill by moving her hands together and quickly pulling them back apart, the movement making the cook blink hard as the money disappeared and then reappeared, "I will give you this fifty dollar bill, no taxes or withholding of any kind

involved, in exchange for five plates of hot food and five
lunch meat sandwiches in a bag for later. I think perhaps
five containers of milk would be appropriate too."

"Do you want coffee?" the man asked, already
moving toward the kitchen door.

Mary smiled and shook her head. "No, thank you,
I don't drink coffee. The milk will be just fine."

"What do you want to eat?" he asked, now standing
with one foot in the kitchen and one outside, holding the
screen door open with his left hand.

"Be creative. Just so it's tasty and hot" she said.
"And quick" she added as an afterthought.

"Give me five seconds" the cook said, the last word
drowned out by the slam of the screen door. He grabbed
five plates from a stack without as much as a glance to see
if he had the right amount.

Mary turned toward the mother and her triplets
and beckoned them with a smile and a wink. "Come on
ladies, lunch is about to be served at somewhere around
the speed of light, so I would suggest you get over here."

The woman opened her mouth to voice a protest
at what she considered unsolicited charity, but her children
ended the debate before it began. They sprinted toward
Mary like she was a magnet and they were made of iron
ore. Smiling at the girls as they hurried toward her, Mary
prepared to pat their pretty little heads after they slid to a
stop in front of her, but they kept going, overshooting their
mark like frisky pups chasing a ball. Mary turned in surprise
as they flashed by and then her surprise turned into a new
smile. The cook was standing behind her, balancing five
heaping dinner plates of beef and noodles along his left arm.

"Easy girls" the cook said, chuckling despite
himself. "There's forks in my shirt pocket. Take one each
and don't spill my good food before you eat a bite of it.
Those are home made noodles too I might add" he yelled at
them as they ran to a patch of grass and dropped in a small
circle, gulping the food like hungry baby bears.

The mother walked over to Mary, wiping her eyes with a handkerchief. The cook raised his eyebrows, making long lines like furrows in a field on his forehead, and offered her a plate of food. She took it from his outstretched hand, nodded slightly, and whispered "Thank you."

"My pleasure little lady" the cook replied, pulling a fork from his pocket and sticking it in the center of the noodles like a flagpole on top of a hill. He offered Mary a plate with one hand and the fork with the other. "And for you Ma'am" he said gently.

Mary took the plate and fork gratefully, the aroma making her stomach growl. "This looks and smells wonderful" she said, sliding a hand into her purse and producing the fifty. "If you don't mind, we'll take the sandwiches as soon as we return the plates. We wouldn't want to miss our bus you know."

The cook stared longingly at the money, sighed heavily, and shook his head. "I don't want your money Ma'am. You see, I should have brought out food to those hungry kids as soon as I saw their mama picking through that garbage can. The truth is, I shamed myself. You enjoy my beef and noodles and I'll make up some sandwiches for later."

He turned toward the kitchen and Mary tapped his shoulder, stopping him in midstride. As he turned back toward her Mary pushed the fifty dollar bill into his shirt pocket. "Those people have no money to buy their food, but I do. That's to pay for what I'm eating and for my sandwich. The rest is a tip for you."

The cook gave her a tired smile and touched his index finger to his eyebrow as a salute. "Ma'am, you are truly an angel on this old rotten earth, and I for one want to thank you for your kindness." He moved away and again opened the kitchen screen door.

"And no mayonnaise on those sandwiches" Mary called after him, "we don't want any spoilage on the bus."

The cook acknowledged her with a wave but didn't turn around.

FIFTEEN

Mary now had four traveling companions and she found the company made the trip go faster. The family moved to the back bench seat with Mary, the three girls falling asleep almost instantly as their full stomachs gave them solace. The girls names were Wilma, Wanda and Waneta, the three W's the choice of their mother, Willimenia. Within minutes of the girls falling asleep, Willimenia began telling Mary her situation, obviously needing a kind ear to pour out her heart.

"My father wanted a boy to carry on his name" she began, almost talking to herself as she shyly explained her unusual name. "I was their first and only child, born after twelve years of marriage, so he figured at that time I would be his only chance. Actually, he was going to name me William, but my mother put her foot down on that one, probably the only time she really defied him at any time in their marriage.

"He at least always called me Willie, which did stick pretty much all my life, probably because it's easier than Willimenia. I prefer it too, so I suppose that my own choice weighs heavily in what I'm called. Don't you suppose?" she said.

"I would think you have every right to choose not only any form of your name you choose but actually any name" Mary agreed, recognizing the woman's lack of self esteem and confidence.

"I never thought of that" Willie said, her face brightening. "Why, I could use the name, oh, maybe the name," she hesitated, then blurted "Mary. I could use your name if I choose." Her face was flushed with excitement at the prospect.

"There is no copyright on a name" Mary said with a gentle smile.

"Well, if I ever changed I would use Mary" Willie said. "But I'll keep my own for now."

"That's fine" Mary said. "Willie is a good name."

"Thank you" Willie said with a relieved sigh. "My husband hated my name, in fact I don't think he used it more than two or three times while we were together. He just called me wife."

"What happened to your husband" Mary prodded.

"He's still in Cleveland I guess" she said, glancing around as if she expected to see him on the bus. "He would get really angry at me and then, well I would make him do things he regretted."

"Do you mean he hurt you?" Mary asked.

Willie squirmed nervously in her seat and then gently moved Waneta's head to ease its uncomfortable tilt. The little girl groaned in her sleep and returned to the same position as before. "You see, I got on his nerves sometimes so he lost his temper and hit me now and then. It was my own fault because I should not have bothered him and made him mad."

"Willie, haven't you talked to someone about this?" Mary asked. No one makes another person angry enough to hit them. If your husband hit you it's because he can't control himself, not because of anything you did wrong."

Willie wiped a tear from her eye with the knuckle of her index finger. She nodded agreement, sighed heavily and looked into Mary's eyes. "I know" she said in a whisper, "it's just hard to say. I think I could have taken the abuse if it were just me, but he started hitting the girls. That made me realize I had to get out of there no matter what the cost."

"So where are you going now" Mary inquired.

"My parents live in Florida, just outside of Clearwater. They don't have much themselves, but they said if I could get us there we can stay with them until I find a job." Willie looked out the window at the traffic flashing by the other direction. "I don't want to live with them either, but I've got to think of the girls. I saved a little money each week, a dime from household money here, a quarter from a trip to the grocery store there, and just put it under a loose board in the bedroom. When I saved up bus fare to get us to Florida and a little more for food we just packed and left. I made a mistake and found out the ticket prices had gone up, so we ran out of money and couldn't buy food. I guess we would have picked through garbage cans until we reached Mom and Dad's place. I've got to say when you saw me I had pretty much hit bottom."

"But you did what you had to do for your children" Mary interjected.

"Oh yes, I don't regret it for a moment" Willie said with emphasis. "Eating garbage for a couple of days is much more tolerable than watching my kids get slapped around. The big thing is, I know we'll be all right. I figure the worst has been done to me so how could anything else take me down now. But then, a rich successful lady like you wouldn't understand that."

Mary smiled and patted Willie's hand. "No, I suppose I wouldn't" she said softly.

They fell silent for a time, Willie feeling tired and unburdened by telling her story. She soon slept, her head rolling gently onto Mary's shoulder. Mary touched her hair with a gentle caress and then just sat as still as possible to permit the tired young mother to rest. The engine droned on, carrying Mary closer to her destiny. She wondered if she would have the courage to get off the bus and enter the tiny world of that dingy trailer park. The answer would come soon as she saw a sign stating, Louisville 10, and her pulse quickened in pace with the bus.

The bus stop was actually not far from the trailer park. Mary was surprised at how clearly she remembered everything. A park bench, it's paint peeling and the weathered wood covered with bird droppings, was still at the same spot where, years ago, Mary stopped to gather her thoughts before continuing her exodus. The bus passed the landmark slowly as it cruised toward the Louisville stop. Mary watched the old bench slide by her window, seeming to beckon to her as it faded from sight.

"Louisville" the driver called out, looking into the two foot rear view mirror to see if anyone was preparing to leave. He raced the motor impatiently, anxious to hurry away as quickly as possible. He frowned with annoyance when Mary waved to him and stood at the back of the bus.

Mary's movement caused Willie to stir and mumble, "No, no, please not the children," her brow knitted in sleep and showing an open mask of pain and fear.

Mary pulled a five dollar bill from her purse, rolled it quickly into a compact cylinder, and stuck it in a pocket of Willie's dress. She hurried down the long aisle, stepping over legs stuck out in her path like exotic looking traps. The bus driver hurried in front of her to reach the underbelly of the bus first, opening it like a surgeon cutting into a patient. He peered at the tangle of bags as if waiting for Mary's to jump out and walk to her.

"Mine is the flowered canvas bag near the bottom" she said helpfully.

The driver glared at her, suspicion covering his face in unmasked distrust. "Do you have a claim check lady?" he growled.

"Yes, it so happens I do" she answered frostily, holding a ticket with the number 0947284 printed in red, "and I trust you will find it matches the flowered canvas bag on the bottom." She pointed at the bag in question, wagging her index finger to increase the man's irritation.

"Alright already" the driver grumbled, throwing bags onto the ground as he dug for Mary's possessions. The muffled sound of glass breaking came from one of the suitcases, followed by the overbearing aroma of cheap cologne. He cursed under his breath and Mary flinched as the smell drifted up to her nostrils. Dragging the flowered bag from the stack, the driver threw it on the ground in front of Mary and glared at her for a moment before he began tossing the luggage carelessly back into the cargo hold. Without another word or as much as a backward glance the drover closed the hatch, climbed on his bus, and roared away.

A small terminal served as the bus station, the dimly lit interior containing a six stool lunch counter, nine storage lockers, and a prim looking man wearing a crisp white shirt and a casino dealer's visor. He sported a pencil thin mustache that curled on each side of his lip in a precise handlebar. A thick coating of mustache wax glistened as the forty watt naked light bulb strained to adequately light the terminal. The attendant smiled as Mary entered, a copper tooth standing out in its diversity against his row of white upper teeth. The fellow's hair was combed straight back, plastered in place by the same wax that held his mustache. If he bumped his head, the hair looked as if it would be in danger of shattering. Thin as a finishing nail, the man looked almost artificial as he stood behind the lunch counter.

When he spoke his voice parodied his appearance as it boomed like a bass drum in a parade. "Hello Ma'am" he rumbled. "Will it be food or a ticket for you today."

Mary's first reaction was to glance around to see from where the voice was coming. She could not believe this commanding sound was booming from this man. Recovering in an instant, she smiled and said, "Neither thank you. I would like to rent a locker to store my bag if I may."

"Oh, of course" he exploded, moving quickly from behind the lunch counter and grabbing the bag from Mary's hand. "We have so few rentals that I tend to forget about them. Here, I'll put your bag in number four." He opened a waist high metal door and pushed the bag into a rectangular space that looked like an air vent. If you come back and I'm not on duty, this will be easier for you to pull the bag out. You know, about waist level and all." He slammed the door closed, turned a key with the number four imprinted on the top, pulled it out and handed it to Mary. "You'll need a dime to get the key to turn. Just drop it in this slot, stick in the key, and turn. It's as simple as that."

"Thank you" Mary said. "I'm not sure how long I will be."

"That doesn't matter in the least" the man answered. "I don't guess I rent one of those lockers a month, so there's no reason you can't leave your bag as long as you like."

Mary thanked him again and walked outside into a bright sunshine. She walked toward the trailer park, using the time to steel her nerves before entering through the narrow passage. She stood across the street and tried to remember every detail when she completed her short walk, her mind's eye seeing the drab metal homes through the memory of a child.

Walking quickly across the road not to avoid traffic, because there was none, but to propel herself forward, Mary rushed past the entrance like she was breaking through an invisible wall of cellophane. The mature trees throughout the park darkened everything like a specter as well as dropping the temperature by ten degrees. A cold breeze blew over her shoulders and Mary shuddered. She felt like Satan had just breathed a sigh of contentment from behind her back. The hairs on her neck prickled and she fought the irrational urge to spin around for a look.

"Are you lost Dearie?" a voice shouted from Mary's left.

She jumped as if touched and looked at a trailer with the same Manager sign outside that had been there years ago. Sitting in an overstuffed leather chair parked under a rusted, tilted awning, sat the most enormous woman Mary had ever seen. Chins rested upon chins layered to the point that her neck molded into her shoulders and head like a solid unit. The woman's upper arms were so fleshy they completely covered her elbows. A tent like dress attempted to cover her but her legs stuck out like bridge supports with sores the size of silver dollars scattered like a shot group down to her feet, which were bare and coated with black grime. A three pound box of chocolates perched on top of her stomach, along with a pile of crumpled empty red candy cups looking like a flag stuck on the crest of a hill. The woman was looking around this small mountain, her chair tilted back and the leg rest lifting her filthy feet.

"Are you the park manager?" Mary asked, trying not to react to the woman's physical appearance.

"In the flesh Honey, and as you can see that means I'm really the manager." The woman cackled at her own humor, the laughter starting an earthquake of fat shimmering all over her body. The little stack of paper candy cups collapsed under the fleshy onslaught, spilling little red soldiers from the box to flutter lifelessly to the floor.

"I'm looking for Myra Parker" Mary said, trying to ignore the humor. "She lived here a number of years ago and I wondered if she or her family stayed."

"A Myra Parker used to live here but she moved about two years ago" the manager said, talking around two chocolate covered caramels in her mouth. "Lived in unit forty seven I think, over near the park."

"Yes, that was it" Mary said excitedly. "Do you know where she lives now?"

"Nope, she went out of here and didn't forward anything. 'Course, most folks don't bother with that anyhow. I imagine as many as not are running from the law or creditors or somethin'." She shrugged, the movement causing the whole box of candy to begin a slide from the mountain top. With amazing speed for a big person the manager caught the box with one hand and plopped it back on her stomach.

"How about a Ray Don Johnson" Mary asked, her mouth dry as she spoke his name. "He lived over by the park too."

"There's no one by that name here, nor has been for at least three years. I know since I come on just two months past three years" the woman said. "I know everyone in the place, since I got to make sure rent comes in on time and all, and I know I never had no Mr. Johnson."

"Do you mind if I walk around for a bit?" Mary asked. "I'd like to see how the place looks."

"Honey, I can't imagine a quality lookin' person like you rentin' one of these rusted out cracker tins, but if you want a look just knock yourself out. If you find an empty, the key will be in the door. Just go in and look around. There sure ain't nothin' to steal." She cackled again, this time holding the candy box before it fell.

Mary walked on without answering, her thoughts on the mobile where she last saw her father sprawled on the floor in a spreading pool of blood. Walking straight to the trailer, once again surprising herself at how vivid her memory was, Mary noticed the key was in the front door, the sign that the trailer was not rented.

She pushed the door open slowly, as if expecting her father to be standing on the other side of the threshold. For an instant she saw him, her Barlow knife sticking out of him like a pump handle, blood coursing down his jeans. Blinking hard and rubbing her eyes for a moment chased the image away, leaving the reality of the dingy front room, looking exactly the same except shabbier.

The kitchen was covered in a thin layer of dust, the cupboards open in proof of their emptiness. Mary moved down the hallway, pausing to enter the bathroom. The tub was stained beyond cosmetic repair, appearing to be decorated with cracks and dirt. The toilet seat hung crookedly with one bolt intact, the lid missing in action. The small Home Sweet Home placard was still in place, the lettering no longer legible, but Mary remembered what had been there.

Carefully she pushed open the door to her father's bedroom, the stained mattress and worn furniture awaiting her gaze as if frozen in time. She stepped in, tiptoeing as if to not awaken the ghosts, and saw a very light, pink stain on the floor at the foot of the bed. Even after all these years the remnants of Ray Don's blood stayed as a sentinel to the events of that day. When she was a little girl Mary's teacher had described a trip to the rooming house across from Ford's theatre where President Lincoln was taken after he was shot. The blood stain on the pillow and sheets of the bed where he lay, his life draining from his body, was still there after those many years. Ray Don's blood, not to be denied, was still there just as was Lincoln's. Someone had tried to scrub it away, but not with very much vigor.

Mary felt strangled, the room seeming to close in around her. Quickly she retraced her steps and went outside, automatically walking to the small park. One leg of the slide had rusted through, tilting the shiny seat on its side and rendering the apparatus inoperable. A few dollars for a new leg would fix it as good as new, once again making life a little more pleasant for the children who lived in this dreary place. She made a mental note to have it fixed herself.

Myra's old home was occupied by an old man with no teeth and wearing a pair of blue work pants and a white undershirt. Flowers grew around the front of his dingy trailer in stark contrast to the rest of their surroundings. He was watering a circle of marigolds as Mary walked up to him.

"Your flowers are lovely" she said, gesturing to his handiwork. "You must have quite the green thumb."

The old man looked up for just a moment, immediately pulling his eyes back to the dented metal sprinkling can in his hand. "I got nothin' to do with this young woman. It's God who makes them grow and gives them color, I just tend them for Him."

"And you tend them well" Mary said with a smile. "I wonder if you might be able to help me. A friend of mine used to live here, Myra Parker, and I wondered if you might know of her family."

"Well, I been here close to two years" the old man said, putting his sprinkling can on a smooth, round rock and then scratched his chin as he spoke. "There was a nice young woman moving out when I came in. She was down on her luck, and of course you can imagine how far down someone would have to be to lose one of these places." He gestured at the shabby trailers.

"Anyway, this girl was just as nice as could be, just said she couldn't pay the rent no more and had to move on. I want to tell you, there wasn't a speck of dust in this trailer when she left. I couldn't find anything to clean, so I just moved my belongings in and that was that. Nice girl, she was. Yep, real nice, real nice."

"Do you know where she went or can you tell me anything that would help me find her" Mary asked.

The old man looked puzzled for a moment, squinted at Mary in thought, then said, "What's that? Where to find her? My lands I haven't the slightest idea. She just packed up her things and off she went." His eyes narrowed slightly as if he just realized he should be suspicious. "Say, are you some kind of bill collector of somethin'? You can't be kin 'cause you're white. She was a nice girl she was, and I'm not about to help no bill collector find her."

"I'm not a bill collector, I'm her friend" Mary said. "We've lost touch and I want to find her, that's all. I'm not blood kin but we kind of thought of each other as sisters."

He smiled, a big toothless grin that made him appear almost cartoonlike. "That's nice that is, that you were close. I had a sister. She died fifteen years ago, but I still miss her."

"Then you know why this is so important to me" Mary pressed. "Myra and I were very close and I want to renew our friendship. This is no trick, I promise you" she added.

After a long pause, the old man seemed to make a decision. He nodded once, a hard shake of the head, and said, "I don't know if this information is still good, but when she left I made mention about how clean the place was. She told me that was from all the cleanin' practice she got at the hotel. I asked her what she meant by that and she says she cleaned rooms for the Argosy Hotel. Now, I don't imagine no one stays at these places forever, but at least that's an ideal where she was a few years ago."

Mary stepped closer and gently touched his shoulder. "Thank you so much for telling me. If I find Myra I'll tell her you helped. May I ask your name?"

"Everyone just calls me Buck" he said, a bit embarrassed, "so's you can just do the same."

"Thank you Buck" Mary said. "And thank you for tending God's flowers."

"I'm pleased He let me for another season" Buck said with a friendly wink. "One of these years they'll be plantin' marigolds on top of me."

"Not for a long time I'm sure. Goodbye Buck."

"Goodbye pretty lady" he said, already turning back to his flowers. "You come visit anytime."

Mary waved as she hurried away, anxious to find the Argosy Hotel. The park manager waved at her as she neared the entrance and yelled, "Did you find one you liked Dearie?"

"No, I'm afraid not" Mary said as she kept moving.

"I told you that you was too high quality for this place" the woman called out. "You ain't lived in a place like this no time in your life I'd bet."

This was the second time a similar comment had been made to her, the first by the woman on the bus, and now by the trailer park manager. Mary found that instead of being offended she was pleased.

SIXTEEN

The Argosy Hotel was a somewhat long two mile walk from the trailer park. Mary didn't take a cab because she didn't want to waste money on what she considered a frivolous luxury, so she looked up the address at a pay phone booth, asked directions at a corner drug store, and started to walk. Located near the industrial section of town, the Argosy was a combination flop house and temporary living quarters for factory workers waiting for their first pay check.

Mary looked in wonderment at the seven story brick building with a large wood sign on its roof. The sign read ARG S because someone had shot so many holes in the lettering that the O and Y were not legible. Two women in short skirts, spiked high heels, and skin tight blouses unbuttoned almost to the waist lounged near the front desk when Mary walked through the open double doors. Both had peroxide blonde hair that looked like straw and the most incredibly bright red lipstick Mary had ever seen accented their full lips.

The desk clerk tried to look interested as she approached, then gave up and yawned. One of the women pushed away from the post she was leaning against and openly stared at Mary, her eyes moving up and down.

"Excuse me" Mary began, addressing the desk clerk.

"Excuse you is right" one of the girls drawled. "There isn't room for more girls here, you see. Thelma here and me hardly make enough to live on nohow, so we don't need some outsider comin' in."

"Shut your mouth Candy" the desk clerk snapped. "You can't be chasing away every female who comes in this place just because you're worried about your territory." Turning to Mary he said, "Now, just what can I help you with Good Lookin'. Are you maybe here to ask for work? If you are, it all goes through me first."

Candy stomped her high heels in anger. "Come on Frankie, you promised there wouldn't be no more competition if I was nice to you. Now I keep up my side of the bargain so what's the deal here."

Mary pushed her fingers against her forehead as if looking for relief from a headache. She dropped her hands, stared angrily at the two bickering people, and snapped, "Stop it, both of you. I don't want a job, and definitely I don't want a job with you." Her glare withered the desk clerk. "I am looking for someone. Her name is Myra Parker, she used to work here, and maybe still does. I just want to find her and then I'll be gone." She paused to calm down for a moment, her silence now scaring the desk clerk even more.

"You, oh, I mean," he stammered, "you mean Myra in housekeeping. She cleans rooms for us."

"Oh yea, Myra" Candy inserted. "She makes sure I have clean sheets after, well, every time. Nice kid. I saw her about twenty minutes ago on the third floor. I would guess if you just look for her service cart setting in the hall you'll pretty much have found her."

Mary's heart pounded in excitement with the news. Myra was here in this very building, just a few floors away. She headed toward the stairs, eager to find her dear friend.

"Hey" the desk clerk shouted.

Mary turned at the stair rail and looked back. "Yes" she said, anxious to be on her way.

"Isn't that info worth a buck or so?" he asked in a whiney voice.

"Grow up and get real jobs" Mary snapped. She went up four stairs, turned and went down again, added "All three of you," then bounded up the stairs.

She paused at the third floor landing to catch her breath and compose herself. Pushing the door open, she saw a dimly lit corridor leading to doors on each side. At the far end, sitting under a burned out EXIT sign, a cleaning cart sat outside an open door. Mary walked quickly down the hallway, stopping at the entrance to the room and peering inside. The carpeting had been worn to the bare floor in high traffic areas, the walls were so scratched they looked like a unique architectural design, and the curtains were yellowed with age.

A black woman wearing a threadbare white uniform was changing the sheets on a swaybacked queen size bed. She was thin from her neck to her breastbone, her chest almost sunken inward. From there downward she spread out like a mound of soft serve ice cream, her waist thick and rolled into wide, fleshy hips. The woman's legs were like stove pipes all the way to her ankles, the size dwarfing her feet even though they were not small. She worked with a determined speed and power, totally immersed in the work she was doing. Her eyebrows were thick and furrowed tight in concentration, her mouth curled down in a frown as she pulled the wrinkles out of a sheet.

Mary stepped into the room, her first impulse to rush over to her friend controlled because she knew it would frighten her. Myra looked completely different now, and Mary supposed she must also. Very softly she said, "Myra."

The woman jumped away from the bed as if she were caught doing something wrong, her eyes round with fear. She looked at Mary in confusion, then said, "Did I do something wrong Ma'am?"

"No, Myra no of course not" Mary quickly said, again restraining her urge to rush forward. "It's me Myra, I'm Mary."

Myra gasped, her knees buckling for a moment before she regained control. "Mary?" she asked. "Mary Johnson?"

"Yes" Mary cried out, the rest of her words choking in her throat.

"You found me" Myra said softly, tears rolling down her cheeks. "You said some day you would find me and you did. Oh Mary, you can never know how often I've thought of you."

The words released Mary's feet and she ran to her friend. They collapsed in each other's arms, laughing and crying like the children they were when they were last together. They both talked at the same time, asking where each had been, where they lived, then laughing instead of answering the question.

Suddenly a voice from the doorway of the room barked out, "What is this I see going on."

Myra froze in terror while Mary turned in curiosity, a broad smile on her face. She saw a woman in a blue dress holding a clip board. Her gray hair was pulled so severely into a bun that her eyes looked oriental. An angry frown accented her wrinkled face, making her appear as a thin troll. She marched into the room like a drill instructor, her black half heels clomping on the thin carpet. Still unaware of any problem, Mary simply said, "I beg your pardon?"

The woman marched past Mary as if she weren't there. She stopped in front of Myra who was cowering in terror against the wall. "Why aren't you working Myra" she shouted, not as a question but a statement. "You are paid to clean these rooms, not to visit with people."

"I'm afraid this is all my fault" Mary began. "You see, I haven't seen Myra for..."

"I really don't care to talk to you or to listen to your drivel" the woman growled, waving her clipboard at Mary in a dismissive gesture. "My issues are with my employee and no one else. Are you a registered guest and is this your room?" The woman's tone dripped with contempt.

"Well, no I'm not" Mary began, "but you see..."

"I don't see anything except my girl standing around instead of working" the woman spat out. "Now, you will leave this room immediately and I will get on with my supervisory duties." She threw the clipboard onto the bed and turned to Myra. "Now, as for you, I'm tired of your kind being lazy and stupid."

That straw broke Mary's control. "Her kind" she gasped, anger and disgust rising like bile in her throat. "Listen you insufferable, bigoted idiot. You're lucky to have a person of Myra's caliber working here, and if I have my way I'm going to fix that in about one minute."

"No, I'll fix it for you" the woman said in a low voice, her teeth clenched tight and her jaw muscled bunched in anger. "This is what insufferable, lazy girls get from me." She lashed her hand forward in an open palm slap aimed at Myra's face. She sneered an evil smile when she saw the fear in Myra's eyes as the hand streaked toward her face.

The blow never landed. Mary's hand blurred even faster, snatching the woman's wrist a bare inch from her friend's cheek. Mary pulled backward as hard as she could, the movement jerking the woman's arm over her shoulder, pulling her off balance, and sent her crashing to the floor. She landed with her legs out straight and her back curved forward and down, which made her end up in a sitting position. A look of shock replaced the sneer on her face, her mouth forcing a perfect O like the angel on top of a Christmas tree.

The room was suddenly silent, Mary and Myra staring down at the supervisor, she staring up at them. After a long moment the woman found her voice and screamed from her seat on the floor, "You are fired. Get out of here now and don't come back. Your pay for the week is forfeited and if either of you ever comes in this hotel again I will immediately call the police."

Mary grabbed Myra's hand and pulled her along toward the door. "Call the police" Mary snapped, "I'm sure they would be interested in talking to the desk clerk and his two girls downstairs." As an afterthought, Mary went back to the bed and picked up the clipboard. It held a thick stack of papers with notes and records of the cleaning done in each room. Holding the clipboard above the woman's lap, Mary released the spring clip and watched the papers flutter down like awkward birds on and around the startled woman. She threw the clipboard on the floor, took two long strides to recover Myra, and pushed her out the door.

They ran down the stairs at a gallop, Mary excited and pleased while Myra was grim faced and frightened. Mary waved at the desk clerk and the two women still waiting for a customer. As they hurried by no words were exchanged. Moments later Mary was walking toward the bus terminal with her arm locked in Myra's, when suddenly Myra burst into tears.

"Myra what on earth is the matter" Mary asked, concerned for her friend.

"Mary, I need that job" Myra sobbed. "Look at me. I never growed up to be the pretty little girl with the kind of figure a man would just die to have. I got to make it on my own and a black woman with a job is about as hard to find as a mound of gold. I lived on the streets for three months after movin' out of that trailer before I found this job. My mama died and her little bit of money was gone in a flash. I ain't likely to find a job again, especially when they call old Miss Prunely back there for a reference."

"Myra that's why I'm here" Mary said. "Do you remember when we agreed to take care of each other if we ever had the chance? Well, I, wait a minute." Mary looked at her friend in disbelief. "Is that woman's name really Miss Prunely?"

"No" Myra laughed through her tears, "her name is Miss Harter. I just always call her Miss Prunely 'cause she's so mean."

Mary hugged Myra hard and shook her head. "Myra, you haven't changed a bit. Now listen. How would you like to be half owner of a diner in Ohio."

The tears stopped as if a faucet was turned off. Myra looked at Mary with an expression that showed both interest in what she said and concern that her friend had lost her senses. "Mary Johnson, you better not be tellin' me that you come all this way to find me, get me fired, and then let me find out you're crazy or somethin'."

"No, no I'm not crazy" Mary exclaimed. "Did you mean it when we agreed to always remember each other and take care of each other if ever we could? Did you mean it?"

"Yes, of course I did" Myra said with conviction. "I thought of you at least once each week after you had to run off, but I never figured either one of us would never do much more than just scratch out a livin'. I always hoped to see you again, but I pretty much knew I'd never be able to help you."

"Well, guess what" Mary said. "I own a diner and I want you to help me run it. Half of everything that comes out of it is yours, that is if you're willing to come to Brecksville with me. You won't be rich or anything, but the diner makes enough to live, and you won't have any more Miss Prunely's to deal with."

Myra was beyond words, her mouth slack as if controlled by a broken spring. With great effort she closed it and then was able to speak. "Do you know what something like that would mean to me Mary? You just described a dream to me, not something that could ever be part of my life."

"Well wake up Honey, because this is the real thing" Mary said and started walking again. When Myra didn't move she called out over her shoulder, "Come on silly, or I'll take it you're going back to beg Miss Prunely for your old job."

Myra ran to catch up, taking Mary's arm in a tight grip. "I go where you go Mary Johnson, you just try to get me off this arm. I'm attached like a Siamese twin from here out."

Mary laughed heartily. "That's great, I can use a twin. First, we go get my bag from the bus station and then we'll get a hotel room. I need to stay a few days to find out how to get my daddy's killing put behind me."

Myra gasped and moved in front of Mary, grabbing her hands and almost jumping up and down in excitement. "Oh my gosh that's right, you don't know."

"Don't know what?" Mary asked.

"Your daddy ain't dead."

SEVENTEEN

The two women continued in silence to the bus terminal, retrieved Mary's bag, then walked to Myra's small apartment in a row of tenement houses that were little more than tar paper shacks. Each time Myra offered to tell the story Mary stopped her, not ready to hear the truth.

Myra gathered her meager belongings and the two friends went to the Resthaven Motel, a modest yet clean place not far from the bus station. "Wait until we have a room and get settled in" Mary said. "I want to set my mind for the news."

"Okay" Myra agreed, "and this motel has a colored section so I can get a room too."

"What on earth are you talking about" Mary asked, her face wearing a puzzled expression.

"My oh my, some things never change." Myra put an arm around her friend and squeezed. "You always were the most naive girl I ever encountered, and I see things haven't changed a bit. Coloreds and whites don't stay in the same part of the motel silly."

"Why, are you better than me or something?" Mary asked.

After a moment Myra realized her friend was serious and she burst out laughing. "You goofy girl. The white rooms are nice, they got hot water and a toilet in each, just like home. We get only cold water and one toilet in the hall for all of us to share."

They approached the entrance to the Resthaven and Mary pulled up short, staring at Myra in disbelief. "That's the stupidest thing I've ever heard. If your room isn't the same as mine, then we don't stay here."

"Think again Mary. This is one of two places in town who have colored rooms at all. Most just don't allow us in. The fact is, the Resthaven is considered progressive."

"Well, I've got an idea" Mary said and walked into the motel's office.

Myra sighed in submission and followed her inside. The office smelled of stale coffee, old cigarette butts, and sweat. The desk clerk wore a confederate flag civil war cap splotched with engine oil and axle grease, and a tan long sleeve shirt with salty white rings of sweat stains from the arm pit to the bottom of his rib cage. Buttons threatened to explode from the front of his shirt where an enormous gut rolled outward like a hidden basketball. Black curly hairs peeked out of the gaps around the buttons and straining fabric. The clerk was young, perhaps in his early thirties, but he looked forty.

Mary gave him a huge smile and tried not to wince at his smell. She sat her bag down and adjusted her skirt primly. "Why, hello sir" she drawled with an exaggerated southern accent, the sir coming out 'suh'.

The desk clerk leaned forward, made a face etched with pain, and expelled a long, deep belch. Garlic and onions mixed with sour mash whiskey joined together in a gaseous stench that any skunk would have been proud to call his own. "What can I do for you" he mumbled.

Mary stood straighter, raised her eyebrows, and in a perfect southern aristocratic drawl said, "Well, first of all I would suggest you improve your manners in front of a lady. Secondly, I would like to procure your finest suite for at least three nights. Third, I would deeply appreciate it if you would make haste in giving me the key as I am positively exhausted."

"Is she with you?" he growled, ignoring her chastisement and pointing at Myra with a stubby finger with grease under the nail.

"Why, but of course" Mary said indignantly

swishing her skirts like a latter day Scarlet O'Hara. "Surely you don't think a lady would be in the position to care for herself. I could absolutely not survive without Myra."

"Well, she can't stay in your room with you" the desk clerk grumbled. "She has to stay in the colored wing."

"Nonsense" Mary said, her lower lip pushing forward in a pout. "I need Myra with me to get water for me at night or to help me with my personal services. She is with me at all times. Surely you can understand me needing my servant."

The southern belle act took effect. The desk clerk scratched his chin in thought and finally said, "Well, the only way I can do it is to rent you two rooms. If you don't have her stay in the colored room I don't want to know about it, but she can't sleep in the other bed in your room, so she'll have to sleep on the floor."

"Of course, I should hope you'd have such standards" Mary said. Besides, when I travel I use two beds. I get uncomfortable during the night and the only way I can rest is to change beds. The floor will be fine for Myra."

The desk clerk narrowed his eyes suspiciously but Mary held a smile filled with sunshine until he finally shrugged and reached for a key. "This is the bridal suite. It's the only fancy room I have and it costs two dollars a night more."

"That's just fine" Mary said. "I just want to get there before I drop." She dramatically put the back of her hand against her forehead.

"Well hurry along then" the room clerk said, looking very uncomfortable and squirming in his chair. When Mary was closing the door after ushering Myra out, she heard the man groan in discomfort and pass gas.

The two women were silent as they walked to their room, opened the door and went inside. The instant Mary threw the deadbolt lock into place she looked at Myra and they dissolved into laughter. "You can sleep on the floor" Mary cried out between whoops of giggles.

"And I'll take care of your every need all night long" Myra mimicked, then fell on a bed, rolling with laughter.

"If that man would have been any more stupid, he could be a house plant" Mary guffawed. "I don't really think he believed me, but he did at least give up."

"I think the real reason you pulled it off was he wanted to believe someone still had a slave. If nothing else he can tell the big story at the next Klan meeting" Myra chuckled, fanning herself with a piece of stationary embossed with the Resthaven logo and coat of arms. "I swear Mary, I haven't laughed since you left. My goodness, I didn't realize how dead empty life had become until you showed up."

Mary stopped laughing, Myra's words bringing her back to the memory of Ray Don and that dreadful day. She went to the other bed, slipped off her shoes, and jumped on top of the bedspread. She pulled out two pillows, fluffed them against the headboard like two giant marshmallows, and leaned her back into their feathery softness. Expelling a held breath, she looked at Myra and nodded her head. "Well, I think I've put this off for just about long enough. If you don't mind, please tell me from the time I left that room just what happened, and don't hide anything from me Myra. I need to know the truth, and I mean all of it."

"That's exactly what you're about to hear" Myra said with feeling, then duplicated on the other bed Mary's position. She turned slightly to look at her while she spoke. Mary looked straight ahead at the blank wall. "I waited about five minutes after you left and then called the police from the phone in Mrs. Truman's trailer. To the best of my knowledge she was one of the only people that had a telephone, plus she was a bit crazy and walked the city all day. She never locked her door, and I guess I don't even know if she had a lock, but half the folks in the place used her telephone any time they wanted. You'd just walk in, call someone up, then leave without her ever knowin' you was there.

"Anyway, I phoned the police and told them there was a dead man in your unit, and I figured that would bring them quick. It did too, 'cause there were four police cars there in maybe five minutes. They went in with their guns drawn, then one of them came running out and made a call on his car radio. Pretty soon an ambulance came and three fellows run in there with a bunch of equipment. A pretty good crowd gathered by then to see what was going on so I was able to join in with them and nobody even noticed.

"After a while they came out carrying your daddy on a cart. I knew he wasn't dead because he didn't have a sheet over his face. They always cover up a dead person's face you know. I moved up to the front of the crowd and listened to these two police men talking, and they said your daddy told them you tried to kill him to keep him from givin' you a whippin". He said you stole money from him and he was about to take a belt to you when you stuck him."

Mary passed a trembling hand over her eyes and looked at Myra. "Then that's why they said in the wanted bulletin that I attacked him first and then ran away."

"I suppose that's it" Myra agreed. "But that's only the beginning. They took him to the hospital where he came nigh to dyin'. The newspapers wrote about it for a couple days then they went on to things more interestin' than you and your daddy.

"Well, the whole thing didn't die down around here. Folks talked about it most every day, and somehow people kept up to date on the whole thing. It turned out your daddy didn't die at all, and when he got better he changed his story. He told the police you didn't stab him, it was a thief who broke in. He said you went off to live with your mama about a week before he was stabbed and he didn't know how they got the idea it was you that done it. The police said that was because he said you done it, and your daddy said he didn't know what they was talkin' about. He said it must have been because he was out of his head. They asked him to call your mama and let you talk to them and he said he didn't know where she lived.

"Well, I don't guess they believed a word he said, but I also don't think they much cared, I mean he lived and all and wasn't helpin' them much, so they pretty much dropped the whole thing."

"Where is he now" Mary asked, swallowing hard to loosen the lump in her throat.

"I don't know Mary. I guess he came back for his things but I didn't see him. After he moved out the trailer park didn't care any more either, so the whole thing just became an old story. If anyone kept trying to find anything new I don't know about it."

"Then you don't think the police have a warrant out for my arrest" Mary said.

"I don't see how, besides after all these years I would guess the time has run out for them to do anything." Myra sat up on the edge of the bed and looked carefully at her friend. "Mary, just let it go and get on with your life. Somehow I can't believe any good will come of carryin' your daddy's old baggage around in your heart."

"I know Myra, but I have to put it all away on my own terms. I need to find Mama and Daddy just to chase away the ghosts. I want to know how it all ends and where I can go from here. Somehow I feel guilty about everything, my mama getting thrown out, my brother runnin' off on his own, and even for what Ray Don did. I know it's stupid, but it's in me and I can't do a solitary thing about what's inside of me."

Myra nodded slowly, not understanding but at least accepting. She moved to a chest of drawers at the end of the room, pulled them open, and then pushed them closed one by one. She reached into the bottom drawer and pulled out a telephone book.

"What are you doing" Mary asked.

"I'm going to look you up a telephone number" Myra said, waving the thick directory. "Or maybe you ought to look it up. I can read some, but I'm not real good at alphabetical order. That old school I went to stayed closed more than it stayed open."

"That's fine, I'll look it up" Mary agreed, "if you'll tell em what I'm looking for."

"There was a girl who worked at the hotel who was accused of killin' one of her customers. She told the police a man climbed in the window while they was, well, you know, and shot him dead in the bed. The killer looked at her, right square in the eyes, and pulled the trigger on Ginger. That was her name. The gun clicked once, then twice, and then a lot of bangin' started on the door. That killer scooted himself out the window fast and then the door broke in. The police arrested Ginger for killin' him."

"But she wouldn't have had a gun" Mary said in surprise.

"That didn't make them no difference. They had a body and they had a killer. Case closed."

"Now I have two questions" Mary said, a puzzled look on her face. "How does the story come out, and what does it have to do with this phone number I'm going to look up."

"I'm comin' to that" Myra said, her eyes sparkling as she warmed to the story. "I'm sure everyone knew Ginger didn't kill that man. He was a regular and gave her some really good tips you see, and he never beat on her or hurt her ever at all, so there was no reason for her to kill this guy. She told the police all that, even admitting taking money from him for a date, because she figured solicitation was a whole lot less trouble than murder. The police look bad when they don't solve cases right away, so they figured it wouldn't be too hard to put away some tramp. Nobody, including a jury, would care anyhow.

"Ginger got this lawyer, he was free because she didn't have any money and the judge picked him out for her, and he was a nice guy who knew she wasn't guilty no way. Well, he decides to find this guy who came in and really did the killing, because Ginger was going down on this no matter what unless he nabbed the real killer."

"Maybe the police could find him" Mary inserted.

Myra snorted and shook her head. "There you go again, being all naive and everything. The police weren't lookin' Mary, just like they never looked for you. They got so many cases that have families and friends and the like breathin' down their backs that someone alone like you and Ginger just goes into the who cares file. It's not that they're bad people or nothin', it's just they work on the hardest problem at the time. You know, the squeaking wheel gets the grease."

"I suppose I should be grateful it's that way" Mary observed, "but I guess it wasn't too good for Ginger."

"It came out for Ginger and in a minute you'll see that it can be good again for you" Myra said. "This lawyer, even though he didn't get paid much for workin' the case, spends some money and hires a detective to find this killer. This guy goes out and finds the guy, recovers the gun, and beats a confession out of him. Ginger gets off, the real killer gets the chair, and the lawyer goes broke." Myra slapped her hands together like she was dusting off flour, and settled back down on the bed with a satisfied smile.

Mary looked at her quizzically for a long moment and then said, "That's a nice story and all Myra, but I still don't know what it has to do with this telephone book."

"Oh my goodness" she laughed, "I was so wrapped up in tellin' you about Ginger I forgot what brought her about in the first place. You see, that detective was a fella named Olnin Butler. He runs a business called AArdvark Investigations. Ginger said he named it AArdvark to get the first listing in the yellow pages. Pretty smart don't you think? It was Olnin Butler what found that killer, so why couldn't he find your daddy, your mama, and your brothers. I don't think he's that cheap but if you can pay for it he can probably do the job."

Mary grinned and made a sour face. "AArdvark? I

don't know Myra, he sounds pretty cheesy to me."

"All I know is he saved Ginger when no one else could" Myra said defensively. "You don't know what he might do unless you talk to him. It sure can't do no harm to talk to the man."

Mary did find that rationale hard to argue with. She looked in the yellow pages and sure enough, under the heading of private detective agencies, the very first listing was AArdvark Investigations. She went to the telephone and dialed the number before she could change her mind.

The phone was answered on the fourth ring, just before Mary was about to hang up. A man's voice, low and beefy, said "AArdvark Investigations."

Mary cleared her throat and said, "May I speak to Mr. Butler please."

"That's me" the voice said.

"Oh" Mary said, wondering how to proceed. "I'm Mary Johnson and I'm trying to locate my father. Do you do that sort of work?"

"Sure" he said.

A man of few words Mary thought to herself. Out loud she said, "I would like to make an appointment to see you if I may."

"Tomorrow morning at nine" Olnin said and hung up.

"I don't know Myra" Mary said as she hung up the telephone. "This seems to be a very strange man."

"Maybe so" Myra countered, but still, what do you have to lose by just talkin' with him?"

"I suppose you're right" Mary agreed. "We'll give it a try."

EIGHTEEN

Mary was going to go back to the motel when she saw the building where AArdvark Investigations was located. Actually she was somewhat concerned about going inside for fear the place would collapse. She once saw a swayback horse which had been worked so hard its spine bent inward, and this building was a structural example of that swayback horse. The ends of the roof were a full four feet higher than the center, the bow shape continuing all the way to the front door. The old wooden door stood ajar, the door frame having long since caved inward to prevent closure.

Standing on the other side of the street, Mary observed that with two upper windows, one window half way down in the middle of the building, and a front door with a window on each side, gave the impression of two eyes, a nose, and a big grin. She felt that the old place was inviting her into its mouth and intended gobbling her into its stomach full of digestive juices.

"Come on Mary" Myra coaxed, pulling on her friend's sleeve in an attempt to produce movement. "If we're late Mr. Butler might refuse to see us."

"I somehow don't believe Mr. Butler has a host of clientele beating down his door" Mary observed. "Besides, I'm not sure that building can take our combined weight. Look at this place Myra."

"Do you want him spendin' your money on some downtown fancy place or do you want him to go on out and find your kin?" Myra chided. "Now quit your lollygagin' around and let's get in there." She walked across the street by herself, pausing on the other side to turn and beckon to her friend. "Do I have to go in there and do this for you? You're goin' to be mighty embarrassed when Mr. Butler calls me in and says 'You know Myra, I don't pretend to understand this, but say hello to your daddy Ray Don'. Now are you comin' or not?"

Mary sighed and reluctantly trudged across the street. She glared at Myra with no conviction and said, "Fine, let's go. At least if this old dump falls on me it will fall on you too."

"Shoot" Myra grumbled, "it'll probably fall on me and you'll be safe under my poor old dead body. They'll pull you out and you'll say some stupid girl just happened to be right by your side to take the ceiling when it fell."

"Oh shut up" Mary said and they giggled.

The old building did seem to gobble them up as they went in, the dingy interior with no working light bulbs seeming to be ominous and a bit frightening. A directory behind a glass case covered with dirt and grime directed them to the second floor. They climbed creaking stairs that occasionally cracked like a gunshot under their combined weight and brought them to a solid wood door to the left of the stair landing with AARDVARK INVESTIGATIONS lettered in white paint on the door. Mary knocked lightly, received no response, knocked harder again to no response, then she shrugged and turned the doorknob.

The door swung open on well oiled hinges to expose a small yet tidy and efficient waiting area. The walls and woodwork were freshly painted a comforting beige, with several Monet prints lending an inexpensive yet tasteful touch. A half wall with a flat, chest high counter ran the length of the room in the rear, a pair of bat wing saloon style doors at the same level permitting access to the next room.

Sitting behind an enormous flat top mahogany desk in the rear of the back room was a smallish, balding man smoking a Camel cigarette. He was waving his hands in the air, chasing cigarette smoke around his head like a mist surrounding a sailor. Mary was not sure if he was trying to get their attention or was simply getting smoke away from his eyes, but Myra apparently took it as an invitation and pushed through the bat wing doors like a gun fighter looking for trouble. Mary just followed her lead and walked through too.

"Ladies, welcome to my home away from home" the man said, his voice even stronger and more commanding than on the phone. He stood in a swift movement that resembled a power lifter performing the first half of a clean and jerk, strode around the desk in four purposeful strides, and held his hand out first to Myra who was in the lead. She shook his hand and then he offered it again to Mary. She liked him immediately because his grip was firm yet not hurtful and he also shook hands with Myra.

"Olnin Butler" he said with an easy smile and genuine graciousness. He was short but very heavily muscled, his narrow waist accenting a wide, solid back. "Please ladies, sit and be comfortable. I would suppose one of you is Mary, and the other is?" He paused and looked from one to the other.

"I'm Mary Johnson" Mary offered, "and this is my dear friend Myra Parker. It was she who suggested I meet with you Mr. Butler."

Olnin nodded thanks to Myra and returned to his seat behind the desk before speaking. "Thank you Myra, I appreciate the recommendation. Nothing beats the kind words of another."

Myra dropped her eyes in embarrassment. "I know a young girl who was falsely accused and you helped her. I guessed if you put enough effort to help out the likes of Ginger, you'd do a bang up job for Mary."

Olnin lit up like a bulb on a Christmas tree. "You know Ginger?" he asked, a smile spreading on his friendly face.

"Well, I ain't seen her for some time" Myra said. "After she got out of jail she came in and got her things, then she said goodbye. She said she was getting out of the business and that she'd starve before going back."

"She sure did change at that" Olnin Butler said with a chuckle. "You see, Ginger and I got married."

"No, you did?" Myra said, a broad grin covering her face as well.

"We did as truthful as if I'm alive right in front of you."

Mary watched, a bemused look on her face, as the two bantered back and forth about Ginger. She knew beyond a doubt that this warm, humorous man was the right choice.

He was saying, "I asked Ginger if she wanted to work here in the office and she said she wanted babies and an office in the church's ladies aid society. The church part was easy because we weren't foolish enough to tell them about Ginger's past, but the baby took about a year to accomplish."

"Ginger's got a baby?" Myra squealed, completely forgetting herself in the excitement.

"She sure does" Olnin beamed, pulling a battered wallet from his pocket and unfurling a plastic pouch full of baby pictures. "Can you believe those eyes? She has her mother's eyes." He glanced up at Mary and blinked hard, realizing he had turned this business meeting into a casual visit. "I'm sorry Ms. Johnson. I'm afraid I let my pride as a father get in the way of my professional obligations."

"That's quite all right Mr. Butler. Actually, your openness makes me feel more confident in your ability to help me. By the way, please call me Mary."

"And I'm Olnin" he said warmly. "I can say this, if you're a friend of Ginger I'll turn this city inside out if need be and we'll find whoever you want."

"I appreciate your enthusiasm Olnin, but I also don't want to mislead you" Mary said. "I've never had the pleasure of meeting your wife, it's my friend Myra here who told me about your detective work on Ginger's behalf."

"I was a chambermaid at the Argosy Hotel" Myra

injected. "Ginger was always extra nice to me and we became good friends."

"And you're also a friend of Mary here" he said with a nod.

"That's right, she's my friend" Myra said with a smile.

"Friend and business associate" Mary added, reminding Myra of their agreement.

"So be it" Olnin said, leaning back in his chair and lighting another Camel with a scratched and dented Zippo lighter. "I still plan to do what it takes to help you ladies. Ginger will be pleased to hear from an old friend Myra, and maybe you and Ginger can spend an evening together while I work on Mary's little problem."

"I'd like that" Myra said.

"I understand you want your father located Mary. Can you give me some details?"

Mary briefed him with as many details as possible, leaving nothing out. Olnin raised his eyebrows a little when she told him about her treatment by Ray Don but he said nothing. He leaned forward in his chair when she talked about the stabbing incident and her flight to Ohio, then he leaned back again as she explained her life at Ruby's.

When she finished he didn't respond for a long time, the silence hanging like wet wallpaper in the air. Finally he said, "Why do you want to find this insufferable creature. My feeling is it's a shame you didn't kill him."

"I guess I need to heal the wounds" Mary said honestly. "I feel like I'm haunted and I want to exorcise the ghosts."

"Very well" Olnin said with a firm shake of his head. "While I'm at it I'll see if there are any old warrants out there for your arrest."

"I don't want Mary to have trouble with the law as a result of all this" Myra interjected, a worried frown crossing her face.

"Not a chance" Olnin reassured. "I've got a friend

who will take care of everything. He'll check the files and there won't be as much as a layer of dust pushed out of place. I promise I won't do anything that causes any new investigations."

"Then let's get started" Mary said as she opened her purse. "How much do you need right now Mr. Butler."

"Olnin" he reminded her, "and I don't want to charge anyone who's a friend of Ginger. I'll just see what I can turn up."

"Olnin, as I said before I don't know your dear wife Ginger" Mary said, "and besides I want to know you're financially dedicated to my case. Please tell me your fee and I will pay it."

Olnin shrugged and nodded in resignation. "Okay, that's fine by me. I get twenty five bucks a day plus expenses. I don't think this should get into too many extra expenses though."

Mary pulled two fifty dollar bills from her purse and placed them side by side on his desk. "If you find my father before this is used up you may keep the difference. If you haven't found him in four days we'll talk about looking a bit longer. You can reach us at our hotel when you have news."

The phone woke them at five o'clock the following morning. Mary started to pick up the receiver but Myra said, "Don't do that, it may be that warthog desk clerk making sure your 'servant' is answering the telephone." Mary stepped away and let Myra pick up the receiver. "Miz Johnson's room" she said in an exaggerated tone.

"Who the devil is this" Olnin Butler barked as he held the telephone in front of his eyes like he could see through the other end of the line.

"It's Myra" she said, visibly startled. "And just who is this?"

"Olnin" he said, again short and to the point on the telephone. "Get Mary on the line will you Myra?"

"Right away" she said and handed the telephone to Mary. "It's Olnin and he wants to talk to you right away."

"This is Mary" she said, wondering what she forgot the day before.

"How soon can you be in my office" he asked.

"Oh, I would guess we can be there in two hours or so" Mary said.

"Make it an hour."

"But Olnin, We've got to get showered and dressed and then it will be an hour anyway to walk it" Mary protested.

"There will be a cab waiting in front of your room in thirty minutes" Olnin barked. "Put on your makeup or whatever you have to do on the way here."

"I don't want to pay for a cab" Mary groaned. "It's such a waste of money."

"Mary, your father is sitting here in my office" Olnin said softly. "I've already called for the cab."

"We'll be ready in fifteen minutes" Mary said and hung up the phone. "Myra, Olnin has found Ray Don. We've got about fifteen minutes each to get ready for a cab that's headed this way." Mary ran into the bathroom and closed the door.

Myra stood by the closed door to help her hear Mary's voice. "Would you rather I not go with you Mary? I mean maybe you'd rather be alone when you see him."

Mary opened the door enough to stick her head out. She looked into Myra's eyes and said with feeling, "Myra, I don't want to do any of this without you, unless you don't want to go."

"Oh no, I want to be with you any time you need me Mary, I just don't want to be in the way."

"Well, you can't be in the way and if I ever want to be on my own I'll say so" Mary said and closed the door.

"Fair enough" Myra said through the hollow core door. "I'll always be there when you need me Mary." She touched the door with the palm of her hand and waited until she heard the shower turn on.

The cab ride was quiet and tense, the two friends holding hands in a show of solidarity but words not being spoken. The driver tried to be chatty, realizing that the friendlier he was the more likely his fare was to give him a tip. Finally even he gave up and drove in silence.

He pulled up in front of the smile face building and simply announced, "This is the place ladies."

Mary paid him, not knowing that a tip was the usual thing to do. She was so preoccupied with her confrontation with Ray Don that the mumbled insults from the cab driver were totally lost to her consciousness. The cab roared away and the two women walked slowly inside.

"Are you okay Honey?" Myra asked, increasing the pressure on Mary's trembling hand. "We can just turn right around, walk out that door that we just came through, and git ourselves out of this town right now. We grab the next bus, hightail it to Ohio, and by this time tomorrow you and me will be slingin' hash at the diner. What do you say we just walk on." Myra pulled gently on Mary's sleeve, trying to get her to reverse directions.

Walking as if she were in a trance, Mary just kept moving forward one step at a time, not answering Myra or moving her head in the least. At the stairs she moved one foot up, then the other, looking like a bride of Dracula in an old horror movie.

"Mary, you answer me right this minute or I'll pick you up and carry you right out of this place myself." Myra pinched her arm hard for emphasis.

Slowly, Mary turned her head and looked at Myra. "Just keep me going okay? I need to face him and get this over with."

Myra sighed and moved ahead. "Alright, but I'm going to tell you right now if he comes on hard to you I'm going to take him down hard myself." She continued on muttering to herself, "He can't be giving one little bit of hard time no more, or he's got Myra Parker wearin' him like a cheap suit. I'll hit him so hard with my right hand he'll beg me to hit him with my left. I'll slap him so hard his shirt will go up and down in back like a window shade. Hard I tell you, I'm on him hard."

Finally AARDVARK INVESTIGATIONS loomed in front of their faces. Myra stopped mumbling and just turned the doorknob and pushed. The door whisked open and they moved silently into the office, automatically heading past the bat wing doors and toward Olnin's desk. He sat there with his usual Camel in hand, a scowl on his face as he waved them forward.

Sitting on a chair near the desk was a figure, nearly bent double and seeming to be folded within itself. As they came closer the sour smell of body odor, cheap wine, urine and vomit cut through the atmosphere like limburger cheese. Mary could see, on closer inspection, that the stinking mess was a person, trembling from head to toe like a leaf fluttering in a storm.

"Lift your head" Olnin commanded, at which the figure complied immediately.   Under the grease, dirt, and illness Mary saw her father's eyes. He opened his mouth and croaked out "Mary."

"Papa" she whispered, unable to move as she stared at the shrunken shell that was once the powerful bully she feared.

Ray Don turned rheumy eyes toward Olnin and held out a shaky hand. "I need a drink" he gasped, a look of pain etched across his face.

Olnin opened a desk drawer and pulled out a bottle of cheap wine. Ray Don snatched it from his hand, clawed the cap off in a frantic gesture, and turned the bottle to his mouth. Loud gulping noises accompanied the rapid emptying of the bottle and Ray Don didn't stop until it was empty. He sighed with relief as the bottle fell from his hand and clunked to the floor. Almost immediately his head sunk to his chest and he began snoring softly.

"He was actually pretty easy to find" Olnin said. "There's a mission on Summit Street that does what they can to help, but your father is pretty far along. A doctor volunteers health care and keeps a medical history on the homeless as best he can, and he gave me the details of Ray Don's condition. He's got severe liver damage, chronic bronchitis, probably brain damage from a gallon of wine or so every day, and a lot of other damage from syphilis. The doctor got penicillin in him when he could, but as often as not your father refused the medication."

"How long has he been on the street" Mary asked, wiping away a tear sliding down her cheek.

"Probably three years at least" Olnin replied. "He's been a heavy drinker for a long time so it's kind of hard to tell, but the mission has record of him for two and a half years. I can tell you this Mary, he's not going to hurt any other little girls anymore. His life revolves around a full bottle of wine. Nothing else matters to him anymore."

"What will happen to him" Mary asked, twisting her hands nervously.

"The cold truth is he won't live much longer no matter what is done." Olnin leaned forward to make sure he had Mary's attention. "On the street he has a very short time to live."

Mary sighed and rubbed her hands on her face like she was trying to get it clean. "Will you do one more thing for me Olnin?"

"Hey, you're paying the freight my dear. Whatever you want me to do I'll go on and do it. You've got three more days on the old meter anyway."

Mary smiled gratefully at him and nodded. "You've done a good job Olnin. In fact I want to talk about my mother and brothers when this is taken care of. But first, I'd like you to find a home for Ray Don where he can be cared for. I don't want him to go to a place that's harmful or mean, it has to be people who will help him."

Olnin scratched his head thoughtfully. "You beat everything do you know that? I expected to find this guy, watch you yell, scream and spit in his face, and then toss him out of here into the nearest gutter. Instead you want to send this guy to a private sanitarium and foot the bill."

"That's pretty much what I want" Mary agreed. "You see, I hated my papa for a lot of years. He caused all of us a lot of pain and did things to me and my mama that he ought to be hung for, but I also learned something else over the years. Hate is worse than a cancer Olnin. It eats not at the body but at the soul which is a lot more important. If I turn my back on kin and I'm able to do something to help then my soul gets a tumor that can't be cut out by any doctor. You just get Ray Don comfortable and have the bills sent to me and I'll be obliged."

Olnin smiled and nodded his head approvingly. "Mary, you're an amazing woman. I'll take care of this today."

"Thank you Olnin" she replied. "Now, if you don't mind I'd like to tell you about my mama and my brothers, because I'd like to find them too. Then, I think Myra and I will catch the next bus to Ohio. I am truly ready to go home."

NINETEEN

Brecksville took on a carnival atmosphere with the news that Mary was coming home. Half the town waited at the bus stop for the Greyhound's arrival and the return of their favorite restaurant owner. Mary was excited and moved to tears, Myra was frightened and restrained.

Accepting the hugs and hand shaking from the huge welcoming committee, Mary quickly pulled Myra by her side and introduced her as the new co-manager of Ruby's Diner. Myra's fear melted as the friendly citizens of Brecksville good naturedly asked her if Mary had retired and would work her to death or playfully demanded that she remember their names the following morning when they came in for their free meal. Through all of the revelry Mary kept looking about for Ed, Stan, and Fred, anxious to see them and tell about her trip.

The crowd finally dwindled, the excitement draining away and the quietness of the downtown taking over. They were standing near the diner, patiently waiting for the others to leave. Her heart accelerated when she saw Ed, his rangy form leaning against the doorframe, his arms crossed just below his badge. Stan waved, his dark blue apron that protected his white shirt from the hardware store's merchandise flapping a salute in the breeze. Fred just smiled, rocking back and forth on his heels like a schoolboy waiting for recess.

Mary grabbed Myra's hand as the last of the well wishers moved away and ran to her favorite friends. Without thinking she fell into Ed's arms, circling his neck with her own arms and kissing his lips. He grunted slightly in surprise, recovered immediately, and kissed her back as he wrapped her in a bear hug.

"Well, I would guess you must be Myra" Stan Kenton said. "If we can pry these two away from each other maybe we can manage proper introductions" he added with a wink.

Mary pulled back, her cheeks flushed with embarrassment and excitement from the kiss, automatically putting her hands to her hair and adjusting it nervously. "I'm sorry, it's just that I'm so excited to see all of you I forgot my manners."

"Well, I can see you're excited about seeing someone" Fred Flannery said with a mischievous twinkle in her eye.

"Oh stop it you two" Mary exclaimed, her embarrassment melting into simple excitement. "You all know this is my dear friend Myra." She turned to each in turn and said, "This is Fred Flannery, Stan Kenton, and Ed Jenkins."

Myra smiled and nodded shyly to each man. They began talking together as one unit, expressing pleasure at her being there and making her feel as welcome as possible. After a few minutes of small talk Mary said, "Hey, let's go in the diner. I feel like I've been away forever and I want to just be inside." She unlocked the door and they filed into the familiar comfort of the restaurant. "Come on Myra, I'll show you where everything is. I'm so excited I feel like getting started like now."

"You can if you want to" Fred said. "I took the liberty of bringing in tomorrow's food. It's in the refrigerators and the cupboards are filled. I brought in an extra supply because that free food idea of yours will bring in the whole town."

"Wonderful" Mary said, spinning around in excitement. "Myra and I can feed the whole state of Ohio. We'll be like two tornadoes in here in the morning won't we Myra?"

"We sure will I'll swear" Myra agreed, getting caught up in Mary's excitement. "Just bring them hungry folks in and we'll feed them till they bust."

"Go on, work and burn out this crazy energy" Ed said. "You're not going to be good for anything else so just get to work. We'll just be out of here so we don't end up in the way. I'm half afraid if something doesn't move it will get thrown in the fryer."

"Well then look out" Mary said with a laugh, already reaching for the first stack of pots and pans. "If you three come back tonight we'll even cook you some supper right here in your own private diner."

"It's a date" Fred declared.

"I'm leaving before she changes her mind" Stan agreed. "I also have some papers for you and Myra to sign Mary. Everything is set up as you asked and Todd Carpenter drew them up."

"Bring them for dinner and we'll celebrate my partnership with Myra" Mary sang out over her shoulder. She was washing potatoes and Myra had begun peeling. She smiled as the familiar squeak of the door came to her ears as the three men walked out.

Myra peeled potatoes with a speed and agility that amazed Mary. This was obviously a person who worked hard and knew how to get a job done well. Seeming to feel Mary's eyes on her, Myra looked at her new partner and smiled. "You know Mary, there is no reason you should feel that based on a children's promise you should be at all obligated to take me in and give me all this. For lands sake, I didn't do a thing to earn any of this."

Mary put an arm around her friend's shoulders, dripping water down her right sleeve. "You know, first of all you have earned this. You were a friend to a little girl that didn't know much more than pain and fear for most of her life. I had my brothers for a while but that was different. Somehow I guess you think differently about them and, I guess you expect things from them. And I don't know if I would be the same person today if it wasn't for you, so you see you have earned half of this diner. Besides, when Ruby died she left everything to me, including a house and an awful lot of money. So lighten up will you?"

"Okay then, I'll lighten up" Myra agreed. "By the way, why don't I get half the house and half the money?"

The two women immediately dissolved into laughter and they went on with their work. What seemed like minutes turned into hours and finally the preparations for the morning rush were complete. They rested at a table near the window, sipping orange juice and waiting for the return of the men. Mary pointed toward the small living quarters in back and frowned. "Instead of you living in that little place, why don't you stay with me at Ruby's old house. I was going to sell it because it's too big for me to rattle around in by myself, but I wouldn't mind if you were there. We can come and go as we please and that will solve my dilemma concerning the house."

"Mary, I wouldn't know what to do in a big house. Shoot fire, you know what the trailer was like and you saw that overgrown cardboard box I was in when you found me. A little room will do me just fine."

"I felt the same way" Mary said, nodding her head in understanding. "That's why I decided to sell the place, since I can't get comfortable in all that space. But if we were together I guess I don't think it would seem, so, well, alone."

Shadows were crossing the tables as evening approached. They didn't have a light burning so as to discourage anyone who might think they were open for business. The mood was quiet and dreamy so the two women spoke softly in mere whispers. Myra's voice was very close to unintelligible when she spoke, but her next words shot through Mary like an electric shock. "You know Mary, it ain't me you should be sharin' that house and your life with. Since you're in love with Sheriff Ed why don't you just let him slip on the ring and be done with it."

Mary jumped to her feet and began pacing back and forth in front of the table. Her shoes snapped on the floor like a soldier marching in precise formation. Her hands twisting in nervous figure eights and she looked at Myra with a wild look in her eyes. "I can't love a man Myra, you know what men did to me. I have nightmares about it almost every night."

Keeping her voice low and soothing, Myra sat as still as a statue and continued on. "It was Ray Don who caused that Mary, him and that pack of animals that live that way. Honey, most men are just regular people like you and me, full of good and just a little touch of bad, but the bad ain't evil bad like your daddy and those men. We're put on this earth to find the right one to spend our life with, and Mary I don't think the one for you is me." She smiled as Mary stropped pacing and looked at her.

"From what you've told me and as far as I can see, you found the man to be with. I think you know it too, you just need to be brave enough to go with it. I think I'll just live in that little old back room in the diner after all. I can come spend an evenin' or two with you once in a while, but if you get lonely I believe that might just be alright."

Mary sat at the table again, the last ray of sunlight from the setting sun drifting over her face like a warm mist. A compressor in a refrigerator under the front counter kicked in, a worn bearing squealing briefly before rolling into action, and the cream for cereal and coffee continued cooling. "Myra, you're right and I know it, but I can not begin to tell you how frightened I am. What if he turns out to be like all the rest? And what if I'm not what he expected and he decides to leave me? I'm not sure I can take those kinds of chances."

Myra sat back in her chair and giggled. "You silly girl you. You've been through grief six ways from last week and your only worry is how to handle a man. If Sheriff Ed turns out to be a bad egg, then you drop him like a bad habit. As far as him not being happy with you, well I don't think the man's a flat faced fool. There is no need to be worried about things that aren't ever goin' to happen."

"I suppose, but maybe there is reason to worry if you've never had reason not to worry" Mary said. She nodded toward the sidewalk outside and smiled fondly. "Here come the men. Look at them Myra, it's like three little boys in grown men's bodies. Except Ed, he seems more serious than most."

The three men were walking side by side, Ed in the center ignoring an argument between Fred and Stan. They reached the door and Ed pulled it open, standing aside as the two men squeezed through simultaneously, their argument continuing.

"I tell you professional wrestling is nothing but entertainment" Fred was saying. "Those fellows get together and decide on what throws to do and who wins and everything. Nobody ever really gets hurt, and if they really did those things they would kill each other."

"I sat ringside at the Iron Mike versus The Death Mask" Stan continued. "I saw Iron Mike pull a nail out of his trunks and ram it in The Death Mask's head. Blood squirted everywhere I tell you, and the old Mask went down like he'd been poleaxed. A doctor came in the ring and pulled that nail out with a pair of pliers. I saw it myself because I wasn't more than five feet from them."

"That was no doctor you idiot" Fred shouted, waving his arms and almost hitting Ed as he strolled in with a bemused look on his face. "They just have people on the payroll who pretend to be whatever they need. In fact, it could have been some other wrestler that wears a mask too, since you wouldn't recognize him if he always wears it to wrestle. Tell me this, was he a big man?"

Doubt clouded Stan's face as he considered this revelation. "Now that you say that, he was a pretty big guy, and those pliers were your regular, garden variety type you'd use at home."

"There you have it" Fred glowered. "You got taken

in by the show, that's all. There's nothing wrong with it, in fact it's a pretty good show, but none of it is real."

"But the blood" Stan mumbled, "and I saw the nail go in his head."

"Oh for goodness sakes I give up" Fred bellowed. "I don't even want to discuss this anymore."

"I'll second that" Ed said, placing a firm hand on each man's shoulder and propelling them into the diner. "I should arrest you both for contributing to the addition of stupidity."

Mary laughed at them and waved toward their table. "Welcome gentlemen. Have a seat here in the moonlight and my associate and I will prepare a hamburger feast fit for a king. Of course you peasants will think you're eating steak" she added and they all laughed.

Mary and Myra worked together and quickly prepared a platter of hamburgers and french fries. Ed and Fred had pulled two tables together and Stan got bottles of soda pop from a cooler. With the table set, the little group sat in preparation to eat their meager dinner. Myra pulled out a chair at an empty table and sat alone.

"What are you doing over there?" Mary asked as they all turned inquisitive looks in her direction.

"Oh, well usually we aren't allowed to sit at the same table as white folks" Myra mumbled, dropping her eyes in embarrassment.

"Well you'll have to get over that one" Ed commanded, "because no one eats until we all sit at the same table." He pushed his plate away to emphasize his position.

"Well, are you sure?" Myra asked hesitantly.

"Of course we're sure" Fred said.

"Get over here" Stan demanded.

Myra moved to their table, a look of wonder on her face. "I don't know quite how to act" she said.

"Just don't spill any ketchup on my uniform" Ed said with a wink as he attacked his sandwich.

Conversation quickly moved to small talk and the incident was forgotten. Myra was part of their little group and everyone knew it was permanent.

The little dinner party broke up early as Mary and Myra knew the morning would be furious and hectic. After making sure Myra was comfortably in her room Mary walked through the quiet diner, locked the front door, and turned to go home. The squad car was waiting at the curb and when she turned his way Ed reached over and pushed open the passenger side door.

Mary walked over and slid onto the seat without a word and pulled the door closed. Ed shifted into drive and pulled away from the curb. "I see you're out on patrol tonight" she said.

"It was a stake out" he answered. "I heard this beautiful but dangerous restaurant owner would be walking down our quiet little streets so I took it upon myself to give her a ride."

"Well, I appreciate not being in any danger" Mary answered. "I know Brecksville can be a pretty dangerous place after dark."

He smiled in the darkness as he slowed to stop in front of Mary's home, the green glow from his dashboard making him look ghoulish. Ed turned off the engine and climbed from the car, reaching Mary's door just as she was pushing it closed. He took her by the hand and they walked slowly to the front door. Crickets chirped noisily in the grass, busily rubbing their powerful back legs together in an attempt to attract an amorous member of the opposite sex.

Ed kissed her, lifting her chin gently and touching his lips tenderly against Mary's willing mouth. He took a step back and looked into her eyes which were shimmering in pools of moonlight. "Shall I come in?" he asked, glancing toward the closed door.

Mary coughed to push her pounding heart out of her throat. "No, I don't think that would be wise" she answered.

"I don't know that I want to be wise right at the moment" he countered and kissed her again.

Mary patted his cheek, then she squeezed it gently between her thumb and index finger. "This time I'll have the common sense. When I throw mine away then it's your turn to stop us."

"Right you are my dear" he said. "Rest well Mary, I'll see you in the morning." He walked quickly toward his car.

Mary unlocked the door and turned to wave. He was pulling away from the curb and waved in return. The house seemed unusually empty that night so Mary hurried to prepare for bed. The sheets were cool and fresh and she was tired, but it took a long time before she drifted into sleep. That night the nightmares did not come.

TWENTY

Bedlam was perhaps an understatement that morning as a line formed half way around the block, making Ruby's Diner the focal point of the town. Mary and Myra fought a losing battle in trying to keep plates full, tables clean, eggs on the griddle, and everybody happy. Necessity forced them to serve sunny side eggs, bacon, and home fried potatoes. Variations were too difficult with the huge crowd.

Most people were good natured and actually had a fine time visiting with people they had not seen in some time. The noise of course was deafening, everyone talking at once and then getting louder as the noise level grew. The next problem was dirty dishes, cups and plates the first casualty as an endless stream of people poured through the door. Myra jumped to the mounds of soap suds and attacked the smears of egg yolk and bacon grease like an Army Ranger on an obstacle course. She whistled a little tune as the clean dishes again outweighed the dirty, and then she jumped back to preparing food. Mary handled clean up, filled plates, and cooked.

They ran out of food by eleven o'clock, serving lunches when the eggs and bacon ran out. The crowd was gone anyway, the last customer being a salesman traveling to Detroit. Myra turned the CLOSED sign over with a grateful sigh. "I swear we maybe did feed at least half the people in this State. I thought you were crazy to look me up after all those years, and now I'm sure of it."

Mary dropped into a chair, sliding her feet free of her shoes with a groan. After years of not owning shoes she was never truly comfortable unless barefoot. "You know Myra, if this is nuts I want to stay this way, because this was more fun than I've had in years. And you know what, I'll bet a lot of those people will come back now that they've had a taste of our cooking."

"I sure as rain hope so, but just not all of them every day, unless of course you plan on adding a few more people to this place."

"And maybe twice the room" Mary added. "No, I'm not dreaming or anything, I don't really expect all these people every day, but it would be nice to see an increase." She wearily pushed out of her chair and moved toward the grill. "I'll start behind the counter if you'll take the dining room. We've got a lot of cleaning to do before tomorrow morning and there's some pretty major restocking to be done too."

"You are a task master" Myra groaned as she moved toward the cleaning supplies. "My poor dogs aren't even barkin' no more, they're growlin' and snappin'. You know, that old bat at the hotel didn't work me this hard, and you know what else?" She stopped and turned toward Mary who was looking at her with some concern.

"What Myra?" she said.

"This has been more fun than I ever had too" Myra said with a broad grin. "I had you goin' though for a minute there didn't I partner?" She laughed and did a little dance as she continued on her way. "Honey, the way I worked before, I would just be getting started. This old diner isn't big enough to put old Myra on the ground."

Mary laughed and shook her head. "Well, I can see I've got some pretty stiff measuring up to do here, and I have a feeling you'll work me half to death, not the other way around."

"Just stay out of my way or I'll mop you up with the rest of the dirt" Myra warned, waving a mop handle she had just retrieved from the cleaning equipment.

Mary stuck her tongue out and started working.

The afternoon flew by and at four o'clock they were done for the day. The only break in the work was for a short visit with Fred Flannery when he delivered the next day's food and supplies. He obviously enjoyed his visits and typically stayed for a cup of coffee before hurrying back to his store.

"Let's sit together out front for a while" Mary suggested to Myra. "It's so pleasant to just watch the world go by and talk with people as they walk past."

"I may sleep instead of talk, but I'm always honored to sit with you Mary Johnson" Myra said and slipped her arm through Mary's. "I can see why you love it here, it just feels safe and clean. Time seems to stand still."

"Ummm" Mary intoned as she opened the door. "Brecksville saved my life, and I don't just mean the people like Ed and Ruby and Fred and Stan, the town itself saved my life." They sat down on two of the six rocking chairs Mary had bought and sat along the front of the diner. When the inside was full the rockers served as a place to relax until a table was free, or some customers just sat and visited after their meal. Mary always sat for some time after she closed the diner and enjoyed the town's atmosphere.

"You see, there is no trouble here. The worst crime we've had since I've been here is a moonshiner that Ed didn't even arrest because his family needs his paycheck from work. A lot of folks don't even lock their doors, and I think everyone leaves their keys in the ignition. Half the people in town don't even own a key ring because they can't find keys for most of the locks they own anyway. Ed said when he was just a boy someone robbed the bank and shot one of the customers when he refused to give up his wallet. The police officer in town at that time didn't even wear a uniform, so the town council did pass a resolution that said the town cop had to drive a marked cruiser with emergency lights, wear a uniform, and always wear a gun. Ed even carries one when he's not on duty although he's never had to draw his weapon on or off duty. The point is I feel safe here after a childhood of being terrified almost all of the time. That's why I like to just sit and relax in my little kingdom of the universe."

Myra yawned, stretched luxuriously, and began to rock slowly. "I feel it too Mary, even though I'm new and all, but I walk on in here and folks are nice to me. I mean I ate supper yesterday with a banker for ding dumb sakes. I would guess the only black girl without a penny to her name that steps up to a banker's table most anywhere else is not there to eat the food but to serve it I'll imagine. I think we'd best just be quiet about this place or a bunch of people will want to move in and then it's ruined, so we'll just keep this to ourselves okay?"

"Okay" Mary said with a chuckle. She nodded to an elderly couple moving slowly along the sidewalk. "Good afternoon Cecil, and how are you today Edna. Can I introduce you to my friend Myra Parker?"

The elderly couple stopped their stroll and nodded to Mary and Myra. "Good afternoon to you ladies as well" Cecil said gallantly, bowing slightly.

"We had the pleasure of meeting Myra yesterday when your bus came in" Edna added, "but for goodness sakes we can't expect you to remember all of us this soon now can we" she said to Myra.

"No Ma'am, but I expect I'll learn as we go on" Myra said with a warm smile.

"I don't believe I saw you two at the diner today" Mary said. "I hope you didn't replace me during the week I was gone."

"Don't be foolish Mary" Cecil insisted. "You're the closest thing I've found that can come close to my Edna's cooking. With her arthritis I don't like to see her work in the kitchen, but she is by far the best cook in the world you know" he said fondly.

"Cecil, if Edna ever opened a restaurant I'd close without argument the same day" Mary said.

"Oh you stop it!" Edna said, her cheeks flushed with pleasure. "We weren't in because we're too old to fight the crowds like you had today Mary. We'll be in tomorrow morning as usual."

"Well then, you just plan on having your complimentary breakfast tomorrow instead" Mary said. "I'll not have regulars not getting the same treatment as one time guests."

"Mary, you're the best in the business" Cecil exclaimed. "We'll see you ladies tomorrow around seven."

Mary and Myra waved goodbye and watched the elderly couple move slowly along the sidewalk, hand in hand. "They are what this town is all about Myra. They celebrated their sixtieth wedding anniversary about three months ago and they walk through the downtown every afternoon rain or shine. Ed drove them home one day last January when the streets were so icy nobody could stand upright, but there they were walking like always. Cecil had already fallen twice and Edna was sure as anything going to go down. Ed had to threaten to arrest them to get them in his cruiser to go home. They made him stop at the drug store on the way which he said was more of a way to save face than anything."

"They do seem nice" Myra mumbled, her chin resting on her breastbone.

"For goodness sakes go on into bed" Mary said with a laugh. "You're going to fall out of that rocker and hurt yourself in a minute."

Myra struggled to her feet, drunken with sleep and fatigue. "I believe you might just be right as rain about that, so I think old Myra will be off." She did pause to wink at Mary as she unlocked the diner to go inside. "Let's have us a go at this again around six tomorrow mornin'. I'll be so ready you'll have to chase me away from your share of the work."

"That's a date" Mary answered, "but don't count on me stopping you from doing my work." She waved as Myra closed the door.

Mary was tired as well but she didn't want the day

to end. She felt that her life was turning a bend in the road, and maybe at long last the path was straight. She rocked contentedly and watched the movements around her, noting that more birds, cats, and dogs were roaming the streets than people.

She dozed for a short time, automatically rocking in her sleep. A sound beside her pulled her back to consciousness so she lifted one eyelid to see what it was. She smiled at Ed who had just eased into the rocker beside her, the creak of his leather utility belt preventing stealth. He smiled in return and patted her hand that rested on the curved arm of her chair. With great effort Mary opened her other eye and drove the nagging request for sleep from her brain.

"Why don't you go on home to bed?" Ed asked. "You'll feel like you've been pulled through a length of stove pipe if you sleep in that chair all night."

"It was just so nice here I hated to move" she said, stretching her arms over her head and yawning. "Myra was smart enough to go on to bed but here I sit just trying to stretch out the day."

"I understand, really good days are like that for me too. Actually, I'm glad I found you here Mary because there's something I want to tell you and if I don't do it now I may lose my nerve." Ed turned his rocker slightly to enable him to look at Mary's face. "I don't want to make this a big thing or get real flowery or anything so I'm just going to go on and say this."

He paused and looked at his feet as if trying to study the reflection in his spit shined shoes. Finally Mary said, "What is it Ed, are you alright?" She leaned forward a bit to look up into his eyes.

Ed sat straight in his chair and took a deep breath. He blew it out and rubbed his palms on his thighs before going on. "Mary, I'm in love with you and it's driving me crazy. I wake up three or four times every night and find myself reaching for you. I decided this is nonsense and I want to marry you so that when I wake up at night you really will be there."

Mary opened her mouth to speak but he held up a hand and shook his head. She closed her mouth and he continued. "Now, I don't want you to feel like you have to decide this second, in fact I'd rather you think about it. I can only make myself give this speech once, so I want you to take it as an open offer. I want to marry you and you just tell me whenever it feels right that you accept my offer. Now have a good night and don't sleep out here till morning." With that he leaped to his feet and walked quickly to his cruiser.

Mary watched in silence as he roared away, then slowly pulled herself to her feet and walked toward home. This was the most wonderful man she had ever met and he surely did deserve to be happy. She stopped walking and stood a moment thinking about that very fact, Ed Jenkins deserved to be happy. Pushing along again for home, Mary realized what the problem was. She still wasn't sure anyone could be happy with her, but she truly did want to try.

TWENTY-ONE

Mary's generosity turned out to be a commercial success as well. The diner's business increased by over fifteen percent as people continued to come back. Mary felt a bit guilty because her motivation had certainly not been a for profit promotion. Truly she just wanted to offer a thank you to the town. Myra reminded her that in a perfect world good deeds are rewarded and in this case Bresckville was very nearly a perfect world. Common sense then indicated that Mary's good thing resulted in more good things.

The days were turning colder so Mary enlisted Ed's help in moving the rocking chairs from the front of the diner to Mary's basement for winter storage. True to his word, Ed never brought up his pledge of love and offer of marriage and Mary had not as yet found the courage to act on the feelings of her heart. Both felt a new and special bond that went beyond friendship but outwardly each acted as just a friend.

Ed was sitting at his usual table one morning, finishing his breakfast and visiting with Myra and Mary as they waited for the morning rush. The door squeaked open with the first customer of the day and Mary turned to greet them. Her smile froze on her lips as she saw Olnin Butler standing just inside the door. With him was a powerfully built young man who was either completely bald or had shaved his head. Mary gave a little cry, her hands flying to her mouth, and whispered "Jeff."

Her oldest brother rushed forward, his arms outstretched, and Mary met him at full speed, their headlong rush almost knocking the breath from her lungs. They clung to each other in an embrace that neither could release, with Mary's head turned and her ear pressing against Jeff's heart. She heard its solid, excited beat and the rhythm poured love and confidence into her body. "Jeff, oh Jeff" she whispered, "it's really you isn't it."

"It's me" he said hoarsely. "I never thought I'd see you again Mary. I did everything I could think of and finally gave up because I didn't know which way to turn."

Finally Mary pushed away to look at him, but they held hands, not wanting to break the contact and let go. "Olnin found you for me didn't he?"

"Yea, but I don't understand how" Jeff said.

"Not a problem really" Olnin quipped. "Say, do you think I could get some of those eggs and potatoes cooking over there? We've had a long drive this morning and I'm about as hungry as a bear."

"You can have all the food in the place" Mary laughed. "You found Jeff you wonderful, fabulous man."

Olnin casually moved toward the plate that a smiling Myra was heaping close to overflowing with food and said, "Be careful now or you'll convince me. Thank you Myra" he added as he accepted the food.

"Olnin found papa for me too" Mary said to Jeff, pulling him to a table and sitting down side by side.

"I know, he took me to the home last night" Jeff replied. "He didn't know who I was, even after I told him. He wears a diaper now Mary, because he can't control his own functions."

"He ruined his brain with alcohol and disease Jeff, and Olnin found him living on the street." Mary shook her head in resignation. "He's never going to get any better but at least he'll have care."

"That was a good thing you did Mary."

"I don't know if good had much to do with it" Mary said, "but it needed done and I had the means to do it. But now I want to hear about you, what you did, where you've been, and what happened to your hair" Mary said, staring at his bald head.

Jeff pulled one of his hands free, allowing Mary to hold tight to the other, and rubbed his skull as if looking for the holes in a bowling ball. "I worked for a chemical plant in West Virginia for a while. They had a spill and I got trapped in it. The only thing that happened as a result of that is I lost all my hair. It's been a lot of years and it's not come back so I suppose it never will."

"Tell me what happened after you left me that night" Mary asked. "Did you really go to work at the mill?"

"That's exactly where I went, and just like I told you no one ever looked for me or inquired one bit. I worked harder than anyone so the foreman at the mill wouldn't want to ask questions and I just lived my life, at least till the mill closed. That's when I went to West Virginia. I was going to work in the coal mines but I couldn't make myself go down in those black holes. It was too much like going into a grave, so I worked at the chemical plant until the spill. They thought I was going to sue them or something so they paid to send me to school."

"Where did you go?" Mary interrupted.

"I went to a high school and passed some tests that gave me a diploma and then I went to Wilmington College, not to far from here, just between Cincinnati and Columbus. Then I went on and got my masters and doctorate at Ohio State."

Mary's mouth fell open in shock. "You're telling me you're a doctor?"

"I have a Ph.D. in literature" he said, embarrassed by her reaction. "I went back to Wilmington and I teach there now."

"My brother the hill boy, a college professor" Mary said more to herself than anyone. "Who would ever believe."

"I know, it's pretty much beyond me too" Jeff agreed. "Of course it would never have happened without that money from the chemical company. But you seem to have done pretty well yourself." He looked around the diner with approval.

"Oh I'm sorry" Mary said, suddenly remembering herself. "Myra, Ed, please come over with us." She introduced them to Jeff and briefly told him her story. When she finished they all fell silent and pondered all of these new revelations.

Olnin was mopping up a last bit of egg yolk with a crust of bread. He ate it with a flourish and drank a glass of orange juice in two large gulps. Not moving to join the others he took a deep breath and cleared his throat. "I have some other news if you'd like to hear it. I don't like to do this since you're all enjoying this little reunion, but there is some unfinished business."

All eyes turned toward Olnin, his solemn words bringing their collective attention to him. "I'm very sorry to have to tell you this but your brothers Ron and Matt were shot and killed by New Orleans police during a bank robbery two years ago. It's believed they were part of a gang that had held up five other banks in a seven month period of time. I wish it wasn't the case but I'm afraid my sources are unimpeachable."

The diner was quiet when Olnin stopped talking, Mary staring at him in disbelief and Jeff dropping his eyes in sorrow. Ed and Myra looked at Mary with sympathy. "I also am sorry to be the one to inform you" Olnin continued, "that your mother passed away five years ago in Hazard, Kentucky. It may help you to know that she worked as a live in cook for a fine family that cared about her and treated her well. She died from a blood clot in her brain that the doctor said was probably there for years, most likely as a result of one of your father's beatings. I truly am sorry but of course you had to know." He stood awkwardly and moved toward the door. "If you'll excuse me I'll let you folks sort all of that out. You call me Mary if I can help." Olnin left the diner, pulling the door closed behind him.

Tears began pouring down Mary's cheeks like water from an open faucet. She didn't make a sound or change her expression in the slightest, only the tears showed her emotion. Jeff looked up, his face too wet with tears. They stared at each other in a silent struggle to find an answer. Ed and Myra touched Mary and Jeff's arm with their hands, giving their caring touch as the only thing they could do.

At last Mary found her voice. "This is bad Jeff, this is so bad. I don't think I can take this any more, the pain all the time."

"Mary, what do you think Mama would say if she were here" Jeff said through his tears. "She would want her children to go on and be happy with their lives. Mama never quit, remember even when he beat her really bad that time, she never quit once. You and I made it Mary, we made it out of that life in hell. Ron and Matt didn't get over it, we did. Especially you Mary, after all that was done to you and you came forth and made it. Mama would want you to live."

Mary stood and opened her arms to them. Ed, Myra and Jeff stood with her and they all folded into each other's embrace. "Shine forth in darkness unto light" Mary said softly.

"What was that?" asked Myra.

"Oh, it's just a favorite passage of mine" Mary said, smiling now through her tears.

"What does it mean" Jeff asked.

"It means you take life as it comes and you live right despite what other people do" she said. "It also means it's time to take an offer I should have accepted a long time ago." She put her head on Ed's shoulder and he choked back a sob.

Mary squeezed tighter and her little circle of family drew tighter around her. Behind her she heard the squeak of the door as the first customers of the day came in, and Mary knew that she would be just fine.

THE END

About the Author

A 1971 graduate of Wilmington College with a B.A. in English, William B. Keller has been a sales professional for twenty nine years. He lives in Worthington, Ohio with his wife Jill and their son, Will.

Other Published Works by
William B. Keller

" The Price "   short story

"Dwarfs and Dreams" short story

"In memory of Lorena" short story

"A Real Thanksgiving" article

Protecting Your Credit" article

"The Tintype Picture"
contest winning short story
(One of four selected two hundred ninety eight entries)

"In Praise of Fairfield Points System" Article

"A Garden of Love" novel

"The Priest in the Park" short story